Reading Water

An Illustrated Guide to Hydrodynamics and the Fly

Reading Water

An Illustrated Guide to Hydrodynamics and the Fly

Darrell Mulch

Frank Amato

PORTLAND

"How we sit in the stream of life is dependent upon our own form as well as the shape of the rocks around us."

Darrell Mulch is a Landscape Architect who lives in Portland, Oregon. He is an avid fly angler who fishes throughout the summer and winter for trout, salmon, and steelhead.

Flies designed and tied by Darrell Mulch

Photography and Illustrations: Darrell Mulch
Back Cover: Frank Amato
Fly Plate Photography: Jim Schollmeyer
Design: Jerry Hutchinson

Softbound ISBN: 1-57188-256-1
Softbound UPC:0-66066-00445-1

Frank Amato Publications, Inc.
P.O. Box 82112, Portland, Oregon 97282
(503) 653-8108
Printed in Hong Kong
1 3 5 7 9 10 8 6 4 2

Contents

Introduction

This book describes a way of luring fish that few of the classics address in depth. It was written to articulate an approach to fly tying and fly fishing based on the behavior of flies in the water rather than "matching the hatch." It was not written to discredit, devalue, or displace traditional techniques but instead, enhance and augment them. It should serve as a valuable adjunct to any fishermen in pursuit of trout, salmon, or steelhead.

The flies described in this book were developed for rivers in the Northwest and other mountainous regions where steep gradients form distinct pools, runs, terraces, pockets, etc. They were also developed to be fished with a floating line and in rivers easily waded. This does not mean, however, that the flies and applications presented are not applicable to other rivers, but one should keep this in mind.

There is not any debate that tying flies is a skill that can produce miniature works of art. The problem arises when the angler tries to catch fish with these flies, for fish do not eat works of art! The fly fisherman must realize that there are many differences between a fly in a vise, and one in the river. The fly in the vise is tied to appeal to its creator. It is viewed from the side, and tied with aesthetics in mind where proportion, scale, and symmetry play a major role. In addition, the fly tier uses dry materials under the influence of air as a medium and gravity as a force.

The fish on the other hand sees the fly in an entirely different light. In a river the fly is often viewed from the back or from below, and as a meal, not a painting. It is seen in a liquid medium where materials appear and behave differently than in air. The greatest difference between a fly in the vise and one in the river however, is movement. The fly is seen over time, and is not presented to a fish as the static image we see in a vise, but instead as an active creature influenced by the forces of water. The fish observes the fly in the context of water in motion and motion in water. Ideally, the fish should see the fly as an active participant which swims in the current, not as inert detritus that happens to float by.

Flies tied and fished using the ideas in this book work without trying to imitate any specific insect hatch. They stimulate fish into striking regardless of their resemblance to anything natural. They are made by incorporating an understanding of the materials used in fly tying and the characteristics of moving water. I call them "ugly flies" because they are tied to catch fish, not fishermen, and their appearance is not always appealing. Their appearance is a reflection of where, when, and how they will be used. Their success in luring fish is a product of the fly's interaction with water. This interaction is the impetus behind the design of each fly. A design that is based upon an approach to fly angling that utilizes the movement of the fly and its parts. An approach I call "hydrodynamics."

Premise

Historically, if one looks at the evolution of fly fishing, you will find that the idea of angling with a representation of an insect came long after the sport and technique had been developed. Five hundred years ago the "fly" was the original version of our present-day lure, a hook tied with bright feathers which could be easily cast using the weight of the line. Basically, it was a wet fly designed and constructed to swim. The "fly" got its name because of its physical similarity to flying insects, but this similarity was simply a consequence of tying feathers on the hook in the most logical and practical way. It was not until hundreds of years later that the technology came about in hook manufacturing and rooster breeding that the fly tier could generate a fly the size and appearance of a number 28 gnat. If one examines the primary intent of those ancient anglers you will find the essence of hydrodynamics. They tied their flies to lure the fish through the fly's movement and had no idea they could catch one by fooling it with a fake *Pteronarcys*.

Remember, hydrodynamics is an approach to fly tying and fly angling involving the behavior of flies in water and it should not be equated with that branch of science known as fluid mechanics. This approach presumes that any fly that presents the fish with an animate image will induce a reaction. Indeed, it is not necessary to replicate living organisms to do this. Spoons, crankbaits, spinners, and metal jigs are evidence of this fact. The parts of a fly do not have to duplicate the particular anatomy of an insect. To be effective, a fly does not require exactly two tails, two eyes, four wings, or six legs. A fish is not an entomologist, a fish cannot even count! It is more important to show the fish an abstract representation of nature, an image that stimulates the instincts of the fish. The challenge for the fly tier/angler is to utilize the right materials in the proper context and apply this to the appropriate circumstance to produce this image, be it subtle or dramatic. The fly needs to speak a language the fish understands, a language that provokes an aggressive conversation.

The following chapters were written to meet this challenge and help the angler comprehend the factors involved in developing and successfully using the "ugly fly".

There are five major characteristics of moving water that form the foundation of hydrodynamic design. They are surface tension, inertia, direction, density, and turbulence. Each of these characteristics provide the fly tier with different avenues of design in which to create flies that interact with water to generate lifelike images. Each of these avenues is manifested as an ugly fly, (a model that represents an ideal). An ugly fly is an archetype, it is not a specific pattern, but instead, it is a fly assembled with an understanding of the nature of materials. In other words, water, especially moving water, will affect the way fly tying materials behave in a river. If one can manipulate this behavior then he or she can present the fish with an animate image.

Surface Tension

Surface tension is a reflection of the cohesive nature of water. It is the result of the interfacial discontinuities between air and water. We can think of it as a type of molecular membrane of elastic film that resists penetration. If an object tries to break through this membrane the surface molecules move to maintain the integrity of the liquid. Cohesion, the force of attraction between like molecules, allows us to construct flies that literally ride on the river's surface even though they might be heavier than water.

Inertia

Inertia is a ramification of current in a river; i.e., the stronger the current the greater inertia water has moving past the fly. It is the force that pushes on those parts of the fly that protrude from the body, especially when the fly is under tension from the line. When these parts are designed to react or respond to this force they will produce a movement, and that movement imparts a lifelike character to the fly.

Direction

Direction, like inertia, is an inherent and inseparable component of current: i.e., moving water has a rate of flow and a place to go. It is this component of current that can be utilized to move the entire fly to create an impression of an active creature. To differentiate between inertia and direction, think of current as wind, and a fly as a sailboat with its bumpers hanging out. The velocity of the wind causes the bumpers to flip-flap but it is the way we orient the sail to the direction of the wind that initiates a vector action in the boat.

Density

Density is a property of water that acts almost like gravity in reverse. Any part of the fly made from a material that has a density less than or equal to that of water tends to rise in this medium. Any part of the fly that has absorbent capabilities is inclined to become suspended in the liquid and move as it moves. Materials such as this complement the density of water, they "breathe".

Turbulence

Turbulence in a river is the result of irregularities in the configuration of the bottom. Due to these irregularities the resistance and deflection of water causes vortices or miniature whirlpools. These whirlpools create a condition where water moves up from the bottom, and generates a type of hydraulic cushion. The faster the river the more pronounced the effect. It is this phenomenon that enables the fly tier to construct flies that seem to float near the bottom and behave in a lifelike manner even though heavily weighted.

Each type of "ugly fly" represents an avenue of design that recognizes and takes advantage of each individual characteristic of moving water in a river. Dimple flies and waking flies take advantage of surface tension, appendage flies- inertia, fin flies- direction, undulate flies- density, and hinged flies-turbulence. Their use is not dependent upon the time of day or season but rather upon the kind of river environment the angler encounters. For example, on a typical Northwest river the angler might fish pools, boulders, bends, slots, holes, pockets, trenches, tailouts, or buckets, and use a different yet prescribed fly for each situation. The construction of these flies is governed by a set of basic methods of composition.

Dimple Flies

Dimple flies are designed to ride on any glasslike surface of a river. They create the illusion of life for the fish by distorting this surface. Seen from underwater the feet of these flies make delicate impressions. These impressions form an image in the mind of the fish and turn a type of mental key that "fits". The fish's brain interprets the "fit" as prey. These flies are most successful when applied with drag-free, upstream applications. Used properly, in the eddies and in the glass behind boulders, they will rise some species of fish no matter what is hatching.

Waking Flies

Waking flies are constructed so that they plane on the molecular membrane of a river, regardless of its texture. Again, their success is derived by generating a powerful illusion. The fish responds to the visual and sonic disturbance rather than a concrete image. Waking flies produce an aggressive pounce from the fish by forming a compression wave in front of the fly, and a wake behind it. They are an extremely valuable tool in three to six feet of water, where the river drops and bends, and where the angler can hold the fly in front of the fish. They work best when floated downstream, and skated across exactly perpendicular to the current.

Appendage Flies

Appendage flies depend upon the inertia of water to move their parts, which causes them to flicker, vibrate, or flutter like the bumpers on the sailboat. The movement of the fly's arms and legs engage the rods in the retina of the fish, and a reflex is initiated which rotates the eyes to bring that movement into central vision. This reflex not only focuses the eyes of the fish upon the fly, but also its resolve. Appendage flies can be designed to function near the bottom in slots and holes, or near the surface in pockets and runs. In situations that demand that the fly drift at the same speed as the current, yet project an animate image, appendage flies are hard to beat.

Fin Flies

Fin flies are made with a stiff planar surface (sail) to take advantage of the direction of the current. Whenever the fly is presented perpendicular or at an angle to the current the entire fly is moved in a pronounced fashion, it banks and swims against the force of the water. The fly's struggle sends a signal to the fish's lateral line, a sensory organ that detects vibration, and this signal can bring about a surge from the fish. Fin flies perform well in fast shallow runs, and bends. They produce their best action when presented downstream of the angler under tension from the line.

Undulate Flies

Undulate flies usually mirror their surroundings, and go with the flow so to speak. They tend to translate the nuances of current into visible action, they slither, pulse, and breathe. This behavior induces the fish to open its gills and inhale the fly. Undulate flies are effective when worked downstream in deep trenches or upstream in tailouts near the surface. They reach their full potential in slower currents regardless of the way the fly is cast and/or fished.

Hinged Flies

Hinged flies are usually designed to swim near the floor of the river where the turbulence there complements their construction and weight. The fact that they can pivot in virtually any direction allows the fly to respond to the vortices in this layer of the river. This articulated movement imparts life to the fly even though it is heavily weighted, they wiggle and dance. They can be constructed to operate in many types of underwater rooms but display their greatest potential in places like buckets. Their optimum use is in heavy water utilizing a gentle tether where they can be dropped and stopped in front of an unsuspecting hog.

Once the fly tier/angler has chosen the type of fly to construct, the circumstance of its use should be considered. For example, the layer of the river, the depth of the water, the speed of the current, the type of underwater room, and the manner in which the fly is to be presented are important. From this consideration the action of the fly can be choreographed and controlled by manipulating the mechanics of its parts. There are five basic methods of composing the materials of the fly to influence this action. They are type, placement, orientation, quantity, and dimension. These methods allow the angler to use materials for each characteristic of moving water that can be adjusted by specific principles of design in order to modify the behavior of the ugly fly.

Essentially, the fly tier is seeking to design flies that are in hydrodynamic harmony with moving water. One must not equate this harmony with streamlined perfection, however, creating a fly that slips by the fish silently and unnoticed. Hydrodynamic harmony is a balance between the mechanics of fly tying materials and the forces they encounter. For example, if one thinks of a flag as a fly material, and the wind as water current, there is a balance that prevails between the velocity of the wind and the wave-like action of the flag. At a certain wind speed there is equilibrium between the force provided by the wind and the tensile strength and weight of the cloth.

Type

The primary method in which one can modify the kind and degree of action of a component in a fly is through the type of material used. Indeed, every material has a nature i.e., it possesses physical properties that have the potential to generate a behavior. Even though materials may exhibit the same nature, the intensity of that nature may differ. For instance, Flashabou and Mylar both flicker when used as appendages, but because mylar is stronger, it takes a greater force to initiate this behavior. In undulate flies the same can be said for herl, marabou, rabbit fur, and calf tail, they all breathe, but at different intensities. With the continual advent of synthetics and development of natural products it behooves the fly angler-tier to identify this nature, and take advantage of it. The angler will find whenever this is accomplished the fly will present a question that the fish will have a hard time not answering.

Placement

The action of the fly is also influenced by the placement of materials on the shank of the hook. Ultimately, this shank is a non-dimensional entity of length which the fly tier can add to or subtract from. For example, the extended Bunny Leech is much longer than the entire hook, while a sparsely tied traditional salmon fly can be less than half the length of the shank. One must not forget that the placement of materials is not stipulated by the fish's artistic sensibilities but by its instinctual reaction to the mechanics of the fly. I am not saying a traditional fly based upon hundreds of years of use has its parts in the wrong place. There is a functional reason a traditional salmon fly resembles an insect i.e., the wings "fins" are on the spine of the fly, and the legs are on the bottom. This is not the result of aesthetics however, but due to hydrodynamics. The fact that the bend of the hook causes an innate weight distribution and fish-hooking requirement necessitates that the fly tier place the bulk of the materials on the top of the shank. These materials

cannot disrupt the natural balance of the hook or the fly will not swim right, i.e., it will tilt to its side and plane to the surface. Materials placed on the bottom of the shank face the dilemma of functioning acceptably yet interfering with the hooking of the fish.

Orientation

There is a definite distinction between the placement of materials on the shank of the hook and the orientation of those materials. Once the fly tier has decided where to place a material, he or she has the option of orienting it with or against the flow of the current. In general, materials that breathe work best oriented with the current, where the natural grain of the material points from the eye to the bend of the hook. Materials used for appendages which are flexible, and extend laterally from the shank, can be tied with a forward orientation to capitalize their potential for movement. Planar elements, such as "fins," should be oriented to capture the directional forces of the water and transfer that energy into motion.

Quantity

Unfortunately, there are not any concise guidelines for estimating the specific quantity of material the fly tier should use. In general, both dry and wet flies should be more heavily dressed in heavy currents, and more lightly dressed in light currents. There is, of course, a critical mass where the action of the material is dependent upon a minimum quantity. This quantity will in turn define the size and weight of the fly. On the other hand, the amount of material used could be subject to the weight of the fly. If for example one must use a 1/12-ounce fly to get to the bottom, all the other proportions would be limited by that parameter. In another case, one might want to design a dry fly based upon the size and strength of the hook, a hook that will not rocket back to its owner a straight and flattened shank.

Ultimately, the most important aspect of quantity is balance, none of the components of the fly should overwhelm the mechanics of another or the fly will not perform correctly. It is a chicken-egg relationship, an enigma perhaps only the fish can truly solve.

Dimension

With the exception of the prime capes that have been developed in the last few centuries, most fly tying materials come in very limited sizes. In general, their width and shape are a given, and the fly designer can only manipulate the mechanics of the material by altering its length. Essentially, the impetus of manipulating the dimension of a material is to control its relative strength. By regulating this strength, the fly tier can tune the parts of the fly to respond to various degrees of intensity of the forces in a river. The fly tier can tune the parts of the fly to sing a melody, a melody we hope the fish will interpret as a siren song.

Commentary

In many instances, tying flies using these methods of composition will produce very "ugly flies". In a vise, undulate flies may end up looking like flaccid amorphous lumps, appendage flies may appear to be tied backwards, fin flies look crude and incomplete, and waking flies often resemble worn-out shaving brushes. Yet, in moving water, these same flies can metamorphose into potent forms of attraction.

For each basic method of composition there are principles of design that are specific for every kind of "ugly fly". These principles of design are based upon a fundamental law of hydrodynamics. In essence, this law is the most rudimentary connection between a particular characteristic of moving water and the materials used in the construction of the fly. This law establishes the beginning of an avenue of design from which the fly tier/angler can create a fly that interacts with water. Whenever the fly tier/angler uses these principles in tying flies, the form of the fly will evolve as a function of its parts. It may be an ugly form but it will be an effective form.

Surface Tension (Fundamental Law)

Any object made from materials or constructed in such a way that resists adhesion–the attractive force between molecules–will reinforce the cohesive properties of water.

Dimple Flies/Waking Flies

There are essentially three distinct categories of materials used in the construction of dimple and waking flies. They are weight distributants, buoyants, and floatants. Materials such as hackle fit in the first category, spun-clipped hair and foam into the second, and fibers both natural and synthetic into the third. In general, buoyants are used in waking flies, and floatants are used in dimple flies.

Type

Weight Distributants

Materials should be stiff to reduce the level of contact with the water to minute points.

Buoyants

Materials should contain hollow pockets and/or be naturally water repellent, i.e., moose are water animals and their hair is superior to that of deer.

Floatants

Materials should have the ability to retain oils which will make the fly hydrophobic and resistant to the adhesive qualities of water. Fibers should be "curly", not straight, so that the oil adheres to the material, much like a child's toy holds the film of a soap bubble.

Placement

Weight Distributants

Regardless of the construction technique used, the placement of materials need to be balanced so that the entire hook rides on or at the surface. For example, a classic wrapped fly requires some sort of tail, not because a fish would not eat an insect that was maimed, but because the fly would not ride on the surface very far without sinking.

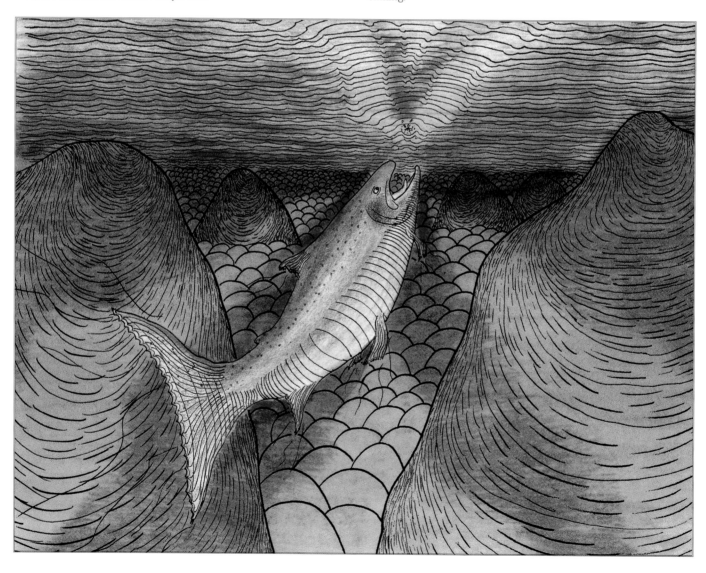

Buoyants

When tying waking flies the buoyant should be placed in the front section of the fly to increase the hydrofoil-like effect generated whenever the fly comes under tension from the line. A buoyant placed near the rear of the fly must not interfere with the hooking potential of the bend of the hook.

Floatants

Ideally these materials should be placed everywhere on the shank of the hook that is not occupied by a weight distributant.

Orientation

Weight Distributants

Spinning hackle so that it is oriented in all directions will distribute the weight of the fly over a larger area and reduce its potential in breaking the surface tension of the liquid.

Buoyants

Spinning hair in all directions serves the same purpose as spinning hackles but also increases the amount of air trapped within the body of the fly.

Floatants

It is best to have fibers criss-cross in every direction to create and interfacial layer of oil and air between the fly and the water, i.e., floatants should be fuzzy, not like a paintbrush, to prevent wicking.

Quantity

Weight Distributants

Simply stated, the amount of material used should be adequate to keep the fly from sinking. Heavier hooks and heavier currents will necessitate the use of more material to accomplish this.

Buoyants

The quantity of any material used as a buoyant in waking flies should be sufficient to return a sunk fly to the surface or prevent it from sinking even in whitewater rapids.

Floatants

Traditional methods of spinning dubbing on the thread mandate one wrap to maximize surface area and avoid compaction of the material. The relationship between most floatant materials and the length/weight of the hook cause a rapid decline in performance with hooks larger than a number twelve.

Dimension

Weight Distributant

To distribute the weight of the fly evenly, the points of contact should fall within the same plane. This can be accomplished with long even hackles that are slightly wider than the gap of the hook.

Buoyants

When using spun-clipped hair, moose, the fly tier should utilize that portion of the shaft that is hollow and not tie flies that exceed this natural parameter.

Floatants

The thickness of the body of the fly should not exceed the width of the inherent curls of the fiber or it will tend to absorb the water rather than repel it.

Caveat

Although dimple flies and waking flies are tied using the same principles of construction, their final appearance will be quite different. Indeed, their appearance is a reflection of the environment in which they are used. Dimple flies are used in delicate upstream applications, and regardless of

how they are tied—e.g., wisp, parachute, palmered, or classic—they should cause only subtle indentations in the membrane of the river. In general, dimple flies require only one spun hackle, and a modicum of other materials to perform well. They work best in the sizes 18 to 14. In contrast, waking flies are used with a downstream application in rough water and their construction warrants an exaggerated utilization of the same principles. They are usually tied with multiple hackles, and spun-clipped moose hair in the sizes 8 to 4. The object of their construction is to produce a fly that disrupts the surface, and disturbs the fish, which is radically different from the seductive role of the dimple fly and its placid enticement.

Inertia (Fundamental Law)

An object that is flexible and possesses a strength proportional to the force applied to it will reciprocate the movement generated by that force.

Appendage Flies

Type
Relatively stiff materials that bend but do not break are ideal for the construction of appendage flies. The stronger the current, the stronger the material should be.

Placement
Materials can be placed virtually anywhere on the shank of the hook so long as one appendage does not interfere with the movements of another.

Orientation
It is all relative, but in most circumstances, weaker materials can be tied at a forward angle to generate a greater latitude of movement which results in a kind of flapping effect. Materials of moderate strength can be tied perpendicular to the shank for a stroking motion, and stronger materials should be tied in a posterior direction to spring in and out.

Quantity

Without exception, the stronger the material, the less one should use in constructing appendages. In general, longer appendages such as arms should be one balanced pair, legs should be two balance pairs, while cilia-like structures need only reasonable balance.

Dimension

The disposition of materials to return to their original position can be utilized to induce movements in the fly, and this disposition can be altered by controlling the relative strength of the material. This strength can be modified by changing the thickness or width of the material, but most often by its length. Ironically, shortening a materially increases its relative strength by reducing the leverage of the

current. As a simple rule of thumb, if a material bends under its own weight in the medium of air, it is probably too long to function properly in a liquid environment.

Direction (Fundamental Law)

An object placed in a current will orient itself in a manner that offers the least resistance to the directional force of that current.

Fin Flies

Type
Materials used to make the fin of a fly should be rigid and impermeable. These properties will enhance the effectiveness of any shape presented to the direction of flow.

Placement
The fin can be placed on either the top or the bottom of the shank but one placed on the bottom would be significantly smaller so as not to interfere with the bend of the hook.

Orientation
A fin should be attached with a vertical orientation to capture the horizontal direction of current, and generate a movement in response to this interaction. In most circumstances a fin placed horizontally will either plane to the surface under tension from the line or flip to its side.

Quantity
The speed at which the fly responds to the directional force of the current depends upon the amount of opposition presented. In general, the greater the surface area the faster the fly will respond. The quantity of material used to construct this area is limited to the weight distribution of the fly. Since most fins will cover a relatively large surface area on top of the shank, this mass should not overwhelm the natural balance of the fly, i.e., the fly must remain in a vertical position to produce the proper action.

Dimension
In most cases, the shape of a fin will be some sort of triangle. The major surface area can be located either anterior, like a shark's dorsal fin or posterior, like a rainbow's. In general, fins made of feathers tend to look more like a shark's, and fins made of synthetics or hair resemble a rainbow's.

Caveat

In the context of this book, the definition of wings and feet will be established to prevent confusion. Although many fishermen refer to structures of a wet fly as wings and feet this book will make the

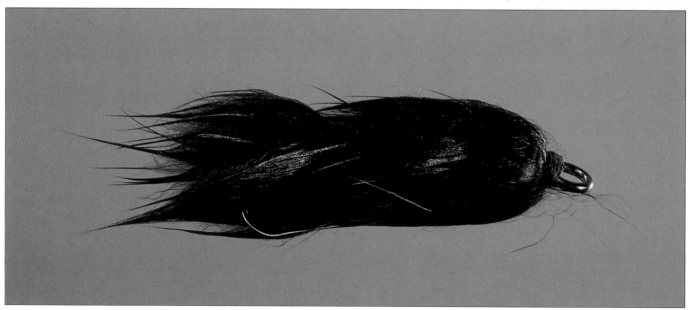

following distinction. Since birds, bats, and insects have wings, an anatomical structure used in flight, only flies that ride on the surface of the water shall possess "wings". Any part of a wet fly that resembles this structure would be referred to as a fin. Also, since insects rest on the surface of the water with their feet, so shall dimple flies and waking flies. Any part of a wet fly that resembles this structure would be considered some sort of appendage such as an arm or leg.

Density (Fundamental Law)
The less resistance an object offers a force it encounters, the greater its capacity for moving with that force.

Undulate Flies
Type
Materials that breathe should complement the forces they encounter. That is, the more subtle the current, the more supple the material needs to be.
Placement
Materials used in making undulate flies work best if placed so that they trail behind the hook. In general, the stiffer the material the closer it should be attached to the front of the fly. For example, bucktail, calf tail, and most synthetics should be tied to the head of the fly, furs to its spine, and marabou feathers to its tail.
Orientation
The grain of the material should be oriented coincident with the direction of the current. Undulate flies reflect the forces around them by flowing with those forces, not by resisting them
Quantity
The materials used in the construction of undulate flies look disproportionately large when dry and in the medium of air, Fluffy Muffies. Yet they look disproportionately small when wet and in the same medium, Gooey Lubies. The amount of material used should reflect this discrepancy, and the fly tier should remember that the density of the liquid suspends and separates these materials.
Dimension
Materials should extend from the shank in a length sufficient to emulate a wave-like action. In most cases, the width-height of the material is a given, and the minimum length needed to generate action is twice this dimension. Also, the stiffer the material is, the longer it needs to be to generate a slithering movement.

Turbulence (Fundamental Law)
An object with an omni-directional hinge will swing in the presence of an omnidirectional force.

Hinged Flies
Type
The materials used in hinged flies should be of adequate weight to sink the fly yet float on the hydraulic cushion of the river's floor. The components that make up the hinge should be loose fittings that cause a minimum of friction.
Placement
The impetus of using a hinged fly is to enhance the action of a weighted fly by increasing its capacity for movement. Its primary components are a weighted head, made from a swivel, an articulated thorax, using the eyes of the swivel and the hook and an abdomen, an extra-long hook reconfigured by bending a new eye.
Orientation
Due to the nature of the materials used, the eye of the head will be oriented horizontally, and the eye of the abdomen will fall in a vertical plane. This will give the abdomen the ability to pivot in any direction.
Quantity
Most of the weight of the fly should be allocated in the head of the fly since it is the tethered section, and is relatively immobile in the first place. This difference in mass between the head and the abdomen will cause the two sections to fall at different rates which gives a dancing action to the fly.
Dimension
The abdomen of the fly should not be shorter than the head or the wiggling movement of the fly will be inhibited.

The Amalgam
Obviously, the fly just described is only a skeleton. It is the addition of other materials that will turn it into a viable life form. These materials should augment the opportunities provided by the hinge by capturing the forces surrounding the fly and transferring them into visible motion. Indeed, most hinged flies are an amalgamation of one or more "ugly flies". They may use fins or appendages to actuate the abdomen of the fly, or the entire fly might be undulate in its composition. In fact, there is not any reason to completely segregate any of the various types of "ugly flies" from one another even though they will perform perfectly well in their purest form. Sometimes the fly tier/angler will want to create a fly based on a blend or fusion of these principles of design. Different pools in contrasting rivers might dictate subtle changes in the design of a fly.

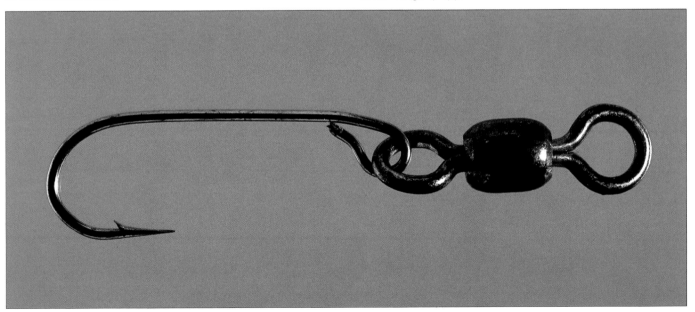

Whenever we decide to construct a fly it is important to realize the parameters of the materials we are using and the conditions for which the fly is created. As you may recall the design of the "ugly fly" is based upon its interaction with water and not its attraction to fishermen. The way the fly looks should not be the result of a preconceived notion but instead its appearance should be derived from the nature of the materials used. Regardless of what kind of material one uses to tie flies, each material has a nature. It possesses physical properties that have the potential to generate a behavior, i.e., skate, flicker, bank, pulse, wiggle, etc. This nature stems from the inherent properties of the material and its relationship to the characteristics of moving water. Usually, this nature is more suited to one type of "ugly fly" than another but some materials can be used in radically different ways. For example, a stiff vane feather can be used either as hackle spun around the shank to support a dimple fly on the surface, or the entire feather can be used as a type of giant arm in an appendage fly.

The schedule on the following page is a categorization of materials and their possible behavior. It is an approximate evaluation, and the way I comprehend and use these materials. Nothing in this schedule is cast in stone nor does it include every material available. This schedule is provided to help the fly tier/angler understand and assemble a fly based upon the principles of design and ideas presented in this book.

Adjunct

Hook: To achieve rapid penetration one may use either a weighted fly or a heavier hook. There are advantages and disadvantages to each of these methods of increasing the speed of sinking or depth of the fly. A weighted fly, in general, will be smaller in diameter and therefore inherently sharper than a heavy hook, such as a 7970, but can lose the natural balance of a heavy hook if weighted indiscriminately. Virtually without exception, a weighted fly should be tied with the bulk of the ballast on the head of the fly. This positioning of the weight will cause the head to sink first and give more life to the fly.

Line: When using sinking flies to get to the floor of the river, the small-diameter leaders will allow the fly to sink faster and further. Six feet of six-pound or eight feet of eight-pound-test leader with four to six feet of butt section is usually adequate to reach fish in six to eight feet of water. In general, the fly angler can expect one quarter of the leader to be consumed by the angle it makes in the water. That is, if the fly is gently walked through a slot, eight feet of leader will penetrate six feet.

Sinker: When using sinking flies the angler is faced with a paradox. Indisputably, a naked hook will sink faster than one that is heavily dressed even though its hydrodynamic potential is minimal. Balance in materials is essential in this circumstance, the fly angler/tier will need to construct the fly so that it gets down to the fish yet provides enough action to generate a response.

Commentary

In some fly fishing circles, one may hear the use of manmade materials is not fair to the fish or somehow a tainted additive to the pure art of fly tying. I find this attitude understandable but in some ways ironic. The expensive capes that have been developed through centuries of breeding are hardly a natural product, and in my opinion they are far superior to any synthetic made today or that will ever be made. In fact, it would be far more equitable to the fish if the fly tier/angler was restricted to using synthetics with their limited properties and applications. I would hate to try to construct a size 18 Baetis imitation without a good grizzly neck. If however, you really want to be fair to the fish, one could demand that a master fly angler use a plastic worm in the midst of a thousand rises!

"Ugly Fly"	Part	Material	Physical Properties	Behavior
Dimple	Feet	Hackle, one (size 18, 16, 14)	Long, stiff, strong and uniform vane feathers where the points of the hackle lie in the same plane when wrapped.	Distribute the weight of the fly to prevent breaking surface tension.
	Body	Dubbing (natural, synthetic)	Fuzzy, water-repellent material that traps air and curls instead of poking holes through the surface membrane.	Resists the adhesive properties of water.
	Tail	Hair, tip (moose)	Durable water-repellent shafts that can be adjusted to any desired length and bent to adjust the tail.	Distribute the weight of the back of the fly to avoid penetration.
	Wing	Vane Feathers (tips)	Large vane feather tips that can be smashed into different configurations without damage to the wings.	Wings pick up wind nuances and transfer vibrations to the feet.
Waking	Feet	Hackle, three (size 8, 6, 4)	Long, stiff, strong and uniform vane feathers where the points of the hackle lie in the same plane when wrapped.	Distribute the weight of the fly to prevent breaking surface tension.
	Body	Hair, base (moose)	Long, hollow, water-repellent shafts that absorb silicon and will not break when spun around the shank.	Return to the surface if sunk and hydroplane when pulled by the line.
	Tail	Hair, tip (moose)	Durable water-repellent shafts that can be adjusted to any desired length and bent to adjust the tail.	Distribute the weight of the back of the fly to avoid penetration.
Appendage	Legs	Rubber	Can be cut to any length desired and the relative strength controlled to complement forces encountered.	Ends of the legs squeeze through the water and vibrate.
		Hackle	Relatively stiff economical vane feathers of various dimensions.	Entire leg tends to ambulate under subtle pressure.
		Mylar Flashabou	Flat, resilient material which can be placed virtually indiscriminately upon shank; Mylar can be longer.	Legs flicker.
		Chenille Herl	When wrapped around shank they can be used in fairly calm-flowing water and in situations where micro-movements are desired.	Cilia caterpillar under subtle pressure.
	Arms	Vane Feathers	Inexpensive, non-uniform feathers which can be cut to place quill on shank and modify its relative stiffness.	Arms flap, especially when the fly changes speed.
Fin	Fin	Contour Feathers Pheasant Tails	Both materials are naturally rigid and planer, and possess an inherent shark shape when attached to top of shank. They can also be sprayed with verathane to increase their effectiveness.	The fin causes the fly to bank when placed perpendicularly to the current, and swim to and fro when swinging across at the end of the drift.
		Krystal Flash	Consistent, constant qualities and quantities that need to be dipped in polyurethane to create a wedge shape.	
Undulate	Tentacles	Herl Yarn	Linear extensions that are usually tied to the front of the hook and whose length and width can be manipulated.	In flowing water these tentacles appear to twist and contort.
		Spey Feathers Partridge Feathers	Essentially, soft-hackle feathers that can be wrapped around front of shank. Spey feathers for large hooks, partridge feathers for small hooks.	Produce a stroking movement of the tentacles when stripped or when the fly changes speed.
		Marabou Rabbit Fur	Can be applied to either the top of the hook or at the end. Marabou can be used on small flies in slow water while rabbit fur only works on big flies in faster water.	Marabou tends to pulse, and rabbit fur tends to slither.
		Calf tail Bucktail	Fairly stiff but pliable materials. Calf tail is shorter and softer, and is used on smaller flies. In general, both materials work best tied on the front of the hook so as to ensure maximum latitude in movement.	Glide through the water in serpentine fashion when swung across the current at the end of the drift.
Hinged	Head	Swivel	Heaviest part of fly, which needs the rings tied with thread to prevent swiveling.	The head dives.
	Thorax	Swivel Ring Eye of Hook	Hook must be re-bent to provide a large eye to integrate with the ring of swivel.	The thorax pivots.
	Abdomen	Hook (extra long)	In general, one should use a hook that is long enough to remain longer than the head of the fly even though it has been re-bent.	The abdomen wiggles.

There are three defined layers in a river for which "ugly flies" are designed. These layers are a byproduct of water and its relationship with the natural environment. In a river, objects and insects either ride on the surface due to the cohesive properties of water, float just under the surface because of their density, or sink to the bottom. These phenomena create natural layers in the river. Fish have evolved with these layers and will respond to stimuli that have a respect for this evolution. These layers should not be confused with the stratification of moving water known as the water column. Technically, they are not discernible layers of water with tangible boundaries but instead, natural consequences of the ecosystem. They are layers of activity in the underwater room of the fish. This room is a space of moving liquid that continually flows by the fish. It has a floor, a ceiling, and a roof. Due to the predilection of the fish to face upstream, and their limited memory, this room has a future and a presence but no past. The fly angler must realize that the fish comprehend this room much differently than we do. They are looking up while we are looking down. To the fish, this room is a contained, tangible, and immediate world. The fish may be able to see, hear, and feel things outside this room but do not actually perceive, or conceive of them. "Out of sight, out of mind."

To the fish, the floor of the river is not the bottom, just as the ground plane is not the bottom of our world. To the fish the surface of the river is not a surface, just as the troposphere is not a surface to us. It is a visual projection of surreal and fluctuating images, a layer that separates their world from ours in both a concrete and metaphysical way. It is their sky!

The Floor

The first layer of the river is an avenue of fluid about two feet in depth, just above the rocks on the bottom. The inhabitants dislodged from the bottom drift in this layer and comprise eighty percent of the fish's diet. From a fish's point of view the floor provides a place to rest both physically and mentally. The structure of the bottom inherently slows heavy

currents and engenders a sense of security to the fish. Big fish establish their favorite "lies" while in this layer and often attack anything that violates their "space", (the length of the fish in any direction). This territorial reaction is the primary reason large "ugly flies" work so well in this layer.

The Vacuum

This layer is a region of varying width between the floor layer and the ceiling layer. In general, it is void of activity, any object with a density less than that of water tends to float above it, and any object with a density greater than that of water sinks below it. It is an area that offers little organic energy, and most objects in this layer are ignored by the fish. From an evolutionary standpoint, the fish does not interpret objects in this layer as food or foe, consequently objects in this layer rarely initiate a feeding or defensive response.

The Ceiling

This layer of the river is approximately six inches in width just below the surface. In it floats anything with a specific gravity equal to or less than that of water. Unfortunate terrestrials that have fallen into the river and aquatic insects in their metamorphic stages become trapped in this layer. Their struggle to break free of its grip make them very vulnerable and the fish take advantage of this fact.

The Roof

This layer of the river is only a few molecules thick and is created by the surface tension of water. It is a membrane which functions as an elastic film that resists penetration. It is a dramatic interface between the fish's world and ours. By looking up at the roof the fish interprets a language from the message it conveys. The ripples, dimples, waves, and wakes speak to the fish and "ugly flies" developed for this layer need to address this issue.

The River's Layers

In a river the current tends to be stratified or laminar. All the water is flowing in the same direction but at different speeds in the form of sheets or ribbons. These ribbons tend to be telescoping in character, and ephemeral in nature. The boundaries between these ribbons fluctuate constantly. This stratification is caused by friction when moving water rubs against the walls of its container. In a river, this container has essentially four walls, the bottom, (river bed), the two sides, (banks), and the top, (atmosphere).

Moving water always finds the path of least resistance, it slides within itself, so to speak. This path is known as the water column, and its location changes as a result of many circumstances but mainly because of depth. In most instances, the deeper the river the greater the atmosphere acts as a wall, and the more the water behaves as if it were in a pipe. In a pipe the water in the very center moves faster than the water next to the walls. In a deep river–eight feet or greater–(this is not an absolute), the water column is also near the center. Water near the surface encounters friction from the atmosphere and slows a little—slows some on the sides, and most on the bottom. The intensity of this effect is quite variable due to the speed of the river. In general, the faster the river, the stronger the effect. In fast deep rivers, fish notoriously hug the bottom where the current is slowest and are reluctant to swim to the upper layers of a river. In slow deep rivers the water column is less rise inhibiting, and a fish will sometimes come to the fly if it has enough "time". Time in this context takes on two dimensions, it has a relationship to the speed at which the fish moves, and it has a relationship to the speed at which the fly moves.

Stratification

From my experience, this "time" is when the rate of the current is about two feet per second or less. It is the rate at which a fish can swim to the surface with little effort. For example, in a river moving at two feet per second, a fish ten feet down would need to see a fly ten feet in front of its lie in order to intercept it.

Remember, fish are lazy and the consumption of energy–(food)–has to exceed the expenditure. Just because a big rainbow can torpedo to twenty five feet per second does not mean it will.

In deep, underwater rooms with velocities greater than two feet per second it behooves the fisherman to use weighted flies that go to the floor of the river. These flies should be as light as possible but heavy enough to reach the fishes level well before they encounter the fish. There is not any real formula for this method of angling since every river is different and no pool is the same. Yet it is a given that the longer the fly stays in the terrain of the fish, the more chance it will generate a response. A weighted fly, that takes three seconds for example, to reach the bottom in perfectly still water will need fifteen feet to reach the same level in a river moving at five feet per second.

In a relatively shallow river–eight feet or less–the water column is shaped much differently than it is in deep rivers. In a shallow river the water column is shaped like a trough and located near the surface. This is because the water in the center remains under the slowing influence of the river bed, and the upper strata glides over the water below. In this situation, the fish will swim to the upper layers if they have time to see the fly, rise easily, and return to their lie. In fact, there is a optimal velocity of current for each circumstance in which the fish has only enough "time" to spot the fly and react. Any fly exceeding this velocity, shooting by overhead, will be ignored, and if the current flows below this velocity the fly faces careful scrutiny and possible rejection. Whenever the current exceeds this velocity an "ugly fly" designed to swing or skate across in front of the fish will often entice the fish to strike.

When an angler decides to pursue fish with an "ugly fly" it is important to understand the opportunities and limitations of each species. The overall demeanor and behavior of each species may be quite different. What they eat, where they lie, and how they react may affect the choice of fly one uses. In general, the more confined any species is, the easier it is to catch it as a function of territory. For example, in confined underwater rooms such as pockets, buckets, steps, or slots the fish become more aggressive because they have no place to go to avoid conflict. Their fight response takes precedence over their flight response. In other rooms, "time" plays a major role in the reaction of the fish. The following species of fish are referred to in this light.

Rainbow, Cutthroat, Brook Trout

In general, these species of fish lie in the same locations, eat the same kinds of food, and react to flies in the same way. Each of these species lie on the outside of the seam or behind a boulder where they can rest and watch things go by. They will rise to the roof of the river for the smallest insects. They can grow to the size of footballs eating gnats! Their main diet however, is usually composed of nymphs taken in the river's floor. In more confined conditions they will attack invaders of their territory. Any type of "ugly fly" can be used to catch these fish if presented to them when they are in the mood.

Dolly Varden ("Bulls")

Bull trout tend to lie in deep slow-moving pools or deep holes and wait for injured or vulnerable fish to drop in. They never rise to a hatch. They will try to eat creatures almost as big as they are in the floor of the river, but usually ignore anything in the ceiling or on the roof of the river. Since they reside in deep holes in small schools their territorial reaction is marginal. In addition, they have a long time to peruse their meal and ignore most of what is presented to them. They are hard to catch! However, big undulate flies, appendage flies, or hinged flies will work in the right conditions.

Browns

Brown trout tend to live in slower and warmer waters than their cousins. One will rarely find them in pocket water or confined conditions. This makes them harder to catch than rainbow and cutthroat but they are not as fickle as bulls. Usually, the bigger the brown trout, the harder it is to seduce to the roof of the river, especially with small flies. Larger meals are therefore required and one should use an "ugly fly" designed to operate in slower water.

Steelhead and Migratory Trout

Steelhead, "migratory rainbows", and other migratory trout almost never take a fly as a feeding response. An exception to this is when they are schooled in big pools, they will sometimes rise at dawn and dusk. Otherwise these fish live off of large fat reserves and do not feed. They are "running" and lie on the inside of the seam in the main channel of the river. They like three to six feet of water where they can rest without being seen. Due to their migration they are sometimes squeezed into small rooms and this is the best time to antagonize them. Any "ugly fly" that violates their space, or even flies that skate across their roof, will cause them to strike.

Pacific Salmon (Coho, Chinook, Sockeye)

Like steelhead, salmon are not hungry, and are even more reluctant to take a fly. They will never take a surface fly but will often grab something with a lot of action if it is delivered to them. In general, this reaction is a function of their age, i.e., time in fresh water. The older the fish the more reluctant it will be to strike. They often travel the same routes as steelhead but typically lie on the outside of the seam and in a little slower water. A hinged fly with lots of action will readily capture chinook in these circumstances provided they are not too dark to respond.

Commentary

In the evolution of the fish, the leader and the hook has been around for only a fraction of time. Fish do perceive these structures as we might think. They are not afraid of being caught by line or hook. Their instinctual memory banks do not conceive of them as a threat. They do not know what angling is! That does not mean however that they will take a fly if they can see the line, for that image often confuses the fish and causes it to reject the fly. Even though fish do not recognize hooks for what they are, the fly tier/angler must not forget that fish do not eat hooks or even artificial flies. They simply grab them and spit them out when they feel the metal, and the larger the hook, the faster this happens. Fish are not stupid.

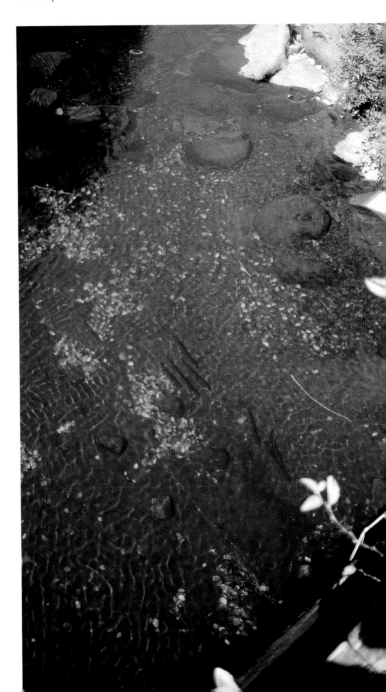

Little Blue Dun

Kingdom	Animal
Phylum	Arthropoda
Class	Insecta
Order	Ephemeroptera
Family	Baetidae
Genus	*Baetis*
Species	*Intermedius*

In the following text there is provided a brief description of aquatic insects in relation to a hydrodynamic approach. This approach is based on using insect imitations to relate to the characteristics of moving water and the opportunistic disposition of resident trout versus "matching the hatch".

In the wide world of fly fishing it is easy to get lost in the volumes of information and details on aquatic insects. If you are not an entomologist or a Latin scholar this information can take a decade to wade through. If one spends much of their time on the water searching for selective trout these volumes are well worth reading. I rarely fish a river from this perspective though, instead I hike up and down the river studying the water and looking for places I know will hold fish yet complement the hydrodynamics of "ugly flies". In the fast-moving streams of mountainous regions it is more important that these flies behave like the naturals than look like them.

Ephemeroptera (Mayflies)

The life cycle of the mayfly is composed of egg, nymph, dun, and spinner. After emerging from the egg, the nymph lives on the bottom of the river for about 350 days. When the time is right, it sheds its nymphal skin, swims to the surface, and emerges as a dun. This dun rides the current until its wings are dry, and then hovers to a tree. It clings to the tree for approximately a day and molts again to become a reproductive adult or spinner. The male and females swarm, mate, and the females return to the river to lay their eggs.

Of all the stages of the mayfly, the dun is the most preyed upon by the trout. Coincidentally it is also the most effective stage to imitate in respect to a hydrodynamic approach. Dimple flies are easy to cast, easy to see, and reveal to the fisherman natural drift or drag. In most circumstances, they should be tied in the sizes 18 to 14. They are effective when fished behind boulders and on the glass-like surfaces of the river regardless of the concentrations of naturals in the area.

Tricoptera (Caddisflies)

The life cycle of the caddisfly is somewhat different from the mayfly's. The caddisfly goes through a complete metamorphosis—egg, larva, pupa, and adult. It spends most of its life in the larval stage encased in a covering of sand or sticks which some call periwinkles. These larvae eventually build a cocoon and go into the pupa' stage for about two weeks. They emerge as adults, swims to the surface, shed a protective membrane and fly to shore. They live as adults for approximately two weeks, swarm, and mate in a distinctive phrenetic bouncing fashion. Then the females return to the river to deposit their eggs in a type of hopscotch dance.

In the life cycle of the caddisfly the most vulnerable time is during its swim to the surface. Unlike the mayfly it does not need to dry its wings, it takes flight almost instantly. An appendage fly used to imitate this stage needs to be presented to the trout so that it drifts in the floor of the river and then rises to the roof when it gets in front of the fish. These flies should be tied in the sizes 12 to 8. Occasionally, a waking fly will work quite well if hundreds of caddisflies are dancing on the surface even though the trout cannot get to them.

Plecoptera (Stoneflies)

The stonefly is the longest lived of the aquatic insects. Some species exist as nymphs for as many as three years before they finally emerge. They crawl onto a rock near shore, break out of their skin and flutter to the nearest branch. They can survive as adults for more than three weeks. After they mate the females deposit their eggs in dive-bomber style or by swimming upstream and across.

Stoneflies are not particularly susceptible to predation at any stage in their life cycle. They are however irresistible to the trout because of their size. Large trout glued to the bottom will move for these flies. A nymph-like appendage fly drifted downstream in the floor of the river will initiate a response, and an appendage fly fished like a spent adult will often cause a trout to come unglued. These flies should be tied in the sizes 6 to 2.

Remember that when the naturals are dislodged from the bottom, they roll tumble, and twist, they do not present the fish with a static image. If that were the case, the advent of the plastic mold would have wiped out fly tying all together.

It is important to consider the fish's mood when approaching a river with an "ugly fly". This mood is a product of the fish's sensory and physical input and the immediate environment in which it resides. Factors such as sunlight, visibility, temperature, and velocity play a major role in this environment, and the actions reactions of the fish. The ambiance created by these factors will affect the type of fly the angler should use.

Sunlight

In the underwater room of the fish, light will affect the way a fish sees, feels, and reacts. Fish, as you may recall, do not have eyelids, and if the sun is pointed in their eyes they are much more difficult to rise to the roof or ceiling of the river. To the fish this light can be blinding, if not simply irritating. In this situation dimple flies or other flies designed to function on the roof of the river are not nearly as effective in sunlight as they are in the shade. Usually a fly designed to operate in the floor of the river will catch fish in bright sunlight but the fish tend to act differently. In bright sunlight most species of fish will move to deeper water and become even more reclusive, sometimes however, they will act contrary to this and move to the shallow head of the pool where they can hide under the froth or white foam. Also since there is so much more light in this situation, the line one uses becomes subject to scrutiny, i.e., three-pound test is as easy to see in sunlight as six-pound test is in the shade.

Visibility

What the fish sees and feels can also be affected by visibility. Conceptually the room of the fish shrinks as the visibility decreases. The fish can see less, and be seen less, which makes it more responsive to the fly. Basically, there are two ways in which visibility can be affected, one is by turbidity, and the other is by rain. Turbidity can be caused by erosion, glacier till, or by aquatic organisms. In general, turbidity is a good thing for the fly tier/angler, so long as the water remains green and the fly is presented close enough to the fish to be seen. Rain also shrinks the room of the fish by breaking up the river's surface texture and visually fractionating the relationship between the fish's world and ours. Whenever visibility decreases, migratory fish such as steelhead will lie in shallower water, and strangely enough, pounce upon waking flies far more readily.

Temperature

The temperature of the water can also affect the actions and reactions of the fish. Since fish are cold blooded their metabolism is dependent upon the temperature of the river. In cold water (water less than 45 degrees) the fish tend to lie in relatively slower water and do not readily move to flies. When they do move, it is at a slower rate than at their favorite temperature of 55 degrees (cool water). The fish will also change the position of their lies when the temperature exceeds 65 degrees (warm water). In this circumstance, they will move into places where the oxygen content is higher, i.e., under foam or froth. They are not as sluggish as when they are frozen but certainly slow down. To briefly recapitulate, a trout or steelhead will move twenty feet for a fly when the water is between 50-60 degrees, but only two feet when the temperature reaches metabolic extremes.

Velocity

With changes in the volume of the water, snow-melt or rain, there will be a concomitant increase in the relative velocity of all sections of the river. This increase in velocity will cause fish, especially migratory fish such as steelhead, to change their lies in the river just as sunlight, visibility, and temperature do. In general, higher velocities cause the fish to move back towards the tail of the pool. An exception to this circumstance is in moderate sized rivers during low flows. A moderate-sized stream is one that is usually knee deep in the tailouts, and can be easily waded. In a moderate-sized stream, migratory fish will move out of the body of the pool and into the head of the pool when the water rises. In this particular case a stream can virtually double its volume before the resultant velocity will push the fish back towards the tail.

In larger rivers, migratory fish run through the head sections of the pool upon the rise in the river level but rarely lie there. Instead, they tend to rest in the four- to six-foot-deep tailouts above any white-water they encounter.

For each type of lie and species of fish, the fly tier/angler should be able to choose a fly that fits the situation. By utilizing the right application, the fly tier/angler can present the fly to the fish in a way that will initiate a feeding or territorial response. Some types of flies, such as appendage flies and undulate flies, will catch any species of fish in the floor of the river. Indeed, big fish, including resident trout, are much more likely to be encountered in this layer of the river, and with these flies than any other application. This does not mean however, that this method is the panacea of fly angling. It is a slow and paced method that will produce one or two fish an hour, maybe. In contrast, other applications using dimple flies might generate ten trout an hour, albeit probably smaller fish, depending upon the species and their concentrations. The same can be said for steelhead, in the right conditions, when there are a lot of running fish in the river, a fin fly fished in the ceiling or a waking fly fished on the roof of the river can be more productive than any type of fly fished in the river's floor. To be the most effective, the fly angler needs to use the right application in the appropriate circumstance. Once the angler learns to read the water, recognize the environmental conditions, and manipulate the fly, this process becomes much easier.

In fact, as the fly angler's experience grows, he/she will find that the pools take on a different meaning. I once returned to a river following a ten-year hiatus and thought that the river had changed, but after a couple of trips realized that it wasn't the river that had changed. It was me!

Commentary

The illustrative diagrams in the following chapter portray fish holding in different types of underwater rooms using both migratory and feeding lies. These diagrams are theoretical representations of possibilities and are not static representations of reality. Each diagram might portray many fish at one time or one fish at many times. Remember that the lie a fish takes in a river will vary depending upon the ambiance of its environment and the particular disposition of each species.

Dimple Flies

Dimple flies are designed to ride on the molecular membrane of the river caused by the surface tension of the liquid. They present the fish with the illusion of life by creating concave impressions in this membrane. They can be constructed in a variety of ways that may or may not resemble anything natural, but their most critical morphology is dependent on resisting the cohesive properties of water. Materials that lift the fly off the water that have hydrophobic properties and distribute the weight of the fly serve this best.

When cast on the roof of the river these impressions caused by the feet of the fly telegraph messages that convey the size, speed, and micro-vibrations of the fly to the fish. In my experience, the fly must remain on the roof of the river drag-free for at least three seconds to initiate a response. A response which very often occurs on the fifth second. Drag is the nemesis of the dimple fly. In most circumstances a dimple fly will be interpreted as food by rainbow, brooks, and cutthroats, but will be ignored by other species. Any place behind boulders or in eddies where the surface is smooth, glasslike, and less than ten feet deep is ideal. A dimple fly presented in this environment should behave like a mayfly dun and be fished in an amicable weather where the water is cool and clear. Usually the angler will want to place the first casts near the rear of the lie and then work forward to reduce the chance of spooking any fish in this area.

There are five basic techniques to present a drag-free dimple fly: snake casting, dead-drift mending, direct opposition, pile casting, and dapping.

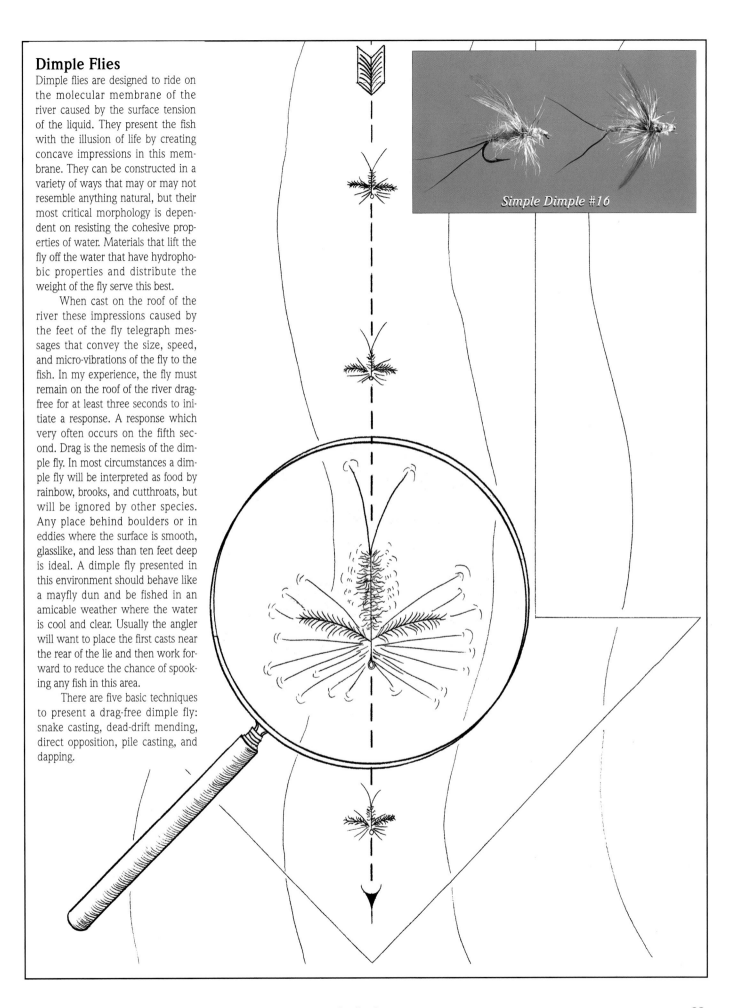

Simple Dimple #16

Waking Flies

Unlike dimple flies, waking flies are designed to take advantage of drag. Whenever they come under tension from the line these flies hydroplane instead of sink. To produce this type of action most waking flies are heavily dressed with multiple hackles and some type of spun hair. Even in white-water these materials should prevent the fly from drowning. When these flies hydroplane they produce waves and wakes on the roof of the river. In water that is relatively shallow these wakes aggravate the fish and that is why they attack these flies with such fervor.

In general, this type of fly is most effective on sea-run cutthroat, steelhead, and most types of resident trout, but will rarely tempt salmon or bull trout. These flies work extremely well wherever the river bends sharply and the angler can position his or herself in a way that enables them to skate the fly directly perpendicular to the current. Steelhead will hit this fly as it approaches the seam and trout tend to take it halfway through the slack water. For some reason this fly works quite well in the rain, perhaps due to the fact that the roof of the river is already agitated or because the fish are holding in relatively shallower lies. There are two basic sinking techniques to present a waking fly: the twitch and the upstream loop.

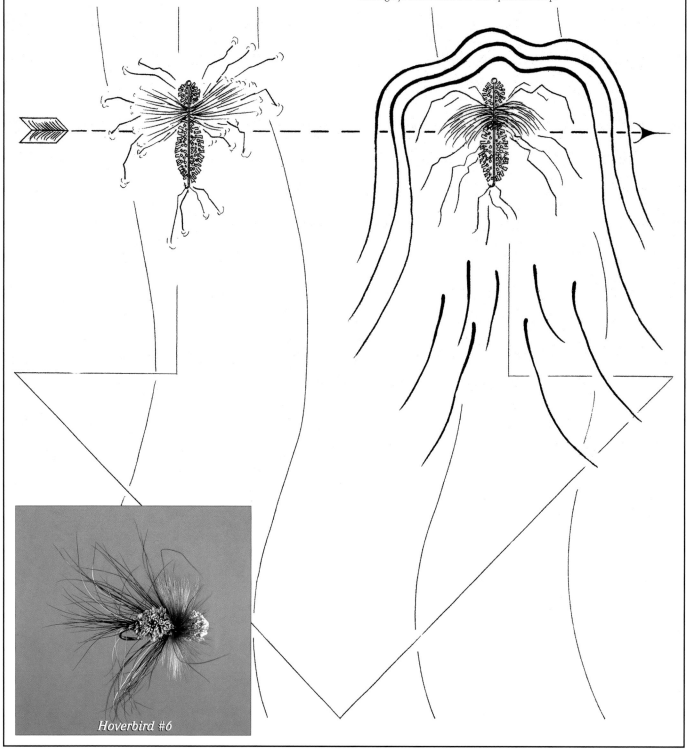

Hoverbird #6

Appendage Flies

Appendage flies are designed to take advantage of the inertia of water. The action produced as a product of this inertia is manifested by the fly's parts and not by the overall motion of the fly itself. Materials that reciprocate the forces they encounter should be used when constructing these flies. For example, when using rubber legs the dimension of these parts should not be too short or too long. Otherwise, they will be too stiff to bend or too weak to return to their original position. That is, they won't vibrate.

Appendage flies can be used in the floor of the river or the ceiling. When using appendage flies designed to function in the ceiling of the river, the fly is usually tied to float near or on the surface. Although the fly may appear to be floating on the roof of the river, its parts are moving within the ceiling and their action is not dependent upon the surface tension of the liquid. In general, appendage flies constructed to sink to the river's floor are used in fairly fast currents, and those constructed to operate in the ceiling are used in somewhat slower currents. Using the appropriate fly in the right current will ensure that the fly has enough time to reach the fish, and the fish has enough time to reach the fly.

Hinged appendage flies such as the Disco Dancer are quite useful in fishing for chinook and steelhead in small rooms such as buckets or pockets, and in linear rooms like slots. Floating flies work best in runs or anyplace that might hold resident trout yet is too rough to be fished with a dimple fly. Often these flies are tied quite large for a variety of reasons. The first reason appendage flies tied for both the floor and the ceiling need to be big is to accommodate the nature of the materials used. The second reason is, a large fly is easier to see when it is partially or completely submerged. The third reason is that a fly of this size and the way it is presented can mimic the struggle of a nymph or adult stonefly, a beetle, or a grasshopper. The final reason for using a fly of this size is that large trout will often hammer a big fly while ignoring numerous tiny ones.

Appendage flies used in the ceiling do not need to be applied in clear water because of their size, but it should be close to the 55-degree optimal temperature. Appendage flies designed for the floor can be used in virtually any condition regardless of its ambiance. There are radically different techniques used in the application of appendage flies, due to the layer of the river they are used in and the construction of the fly. Techniques used in the river's floor are jigging, walking the dog, and the hook shot toss. Techniques used in the river's ceiling are, direct opposition, the roll cast, and the caddis rise.

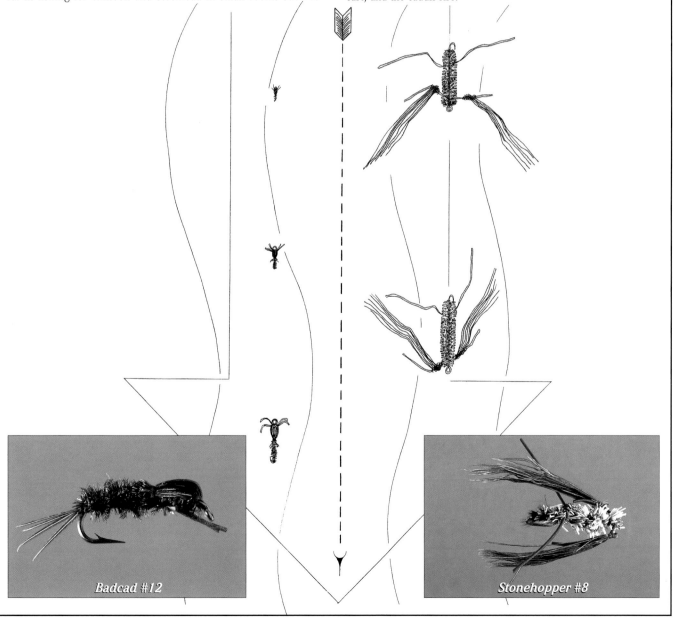

Badcad #12

Stonehopper #8

Fin Flies

Fin flies utilize the direction of moving water to produce movement in the fly. By constructing the fly with a planar surface it will orient itself in such a way as to offer the least amount of resistance to the current, and this attitude adjustment will look much like the swimming of a dace. The surface of the fin should be stiff and impermeable to provide the best action in the fly. In most circumstances fin flies are used in the ceiling of the river where the water is relatively shallow and the fly can be swung in front of a lie. These flies will tempt most species of resident trout, sea-run cutthroat, and steelhead. Salmon and bull trout may respond to this type of fly but it would have to be presented in the river's floor and these species of fish tend to lie in the underwater rooms that do not complement the hydrodynamics of a fin fly. Fin flies work best in fast shallow runs, bends and steps when the water is slightly off color and the temperature of the water is between fifty and sixty degrees. There are four basic techniques that can be used to present a fin fly: the reach cast, modified greased line, the upstream loop, and the swing.

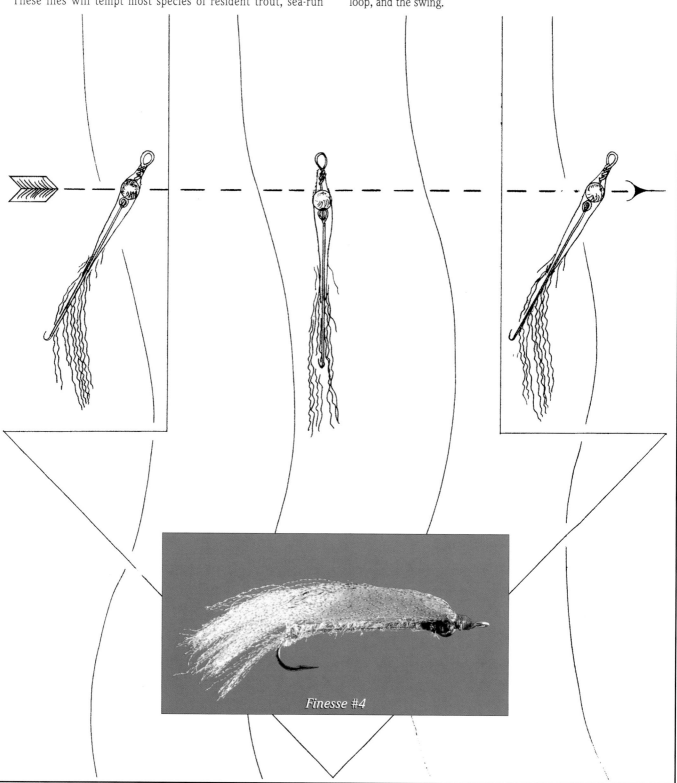

Finesse #4

Undulate Flies

Undulate flies take advantage of the density of water to produce action in the fly. Because their parts are suspended in the liquid, these flies exhibit whatever nuances the current has to offer. These parts should be made of materials that match the intensity of whatever forces they encounter, and be arranged so that they do not interfere with each other's movements. Undulate flies can be used in either the ceiling or floor of the river, and reach their full potential in slow currents where the fish have a long time to peruse the fly. They can be used in deep holes, pools, and trenches or along escarpments, an environment where other types of flies show poorly. Undulate flies designed for the floor of the river will catch fish in almost any water condition, but those designed for the ceiling should be used in clear, slow, and cool water. There are two techniques that the angler should learn to present these flies in the floor of the river. They are: the arc and dredging. Direct opposition and the strip are techniques that should be used in the ceiling of the river.

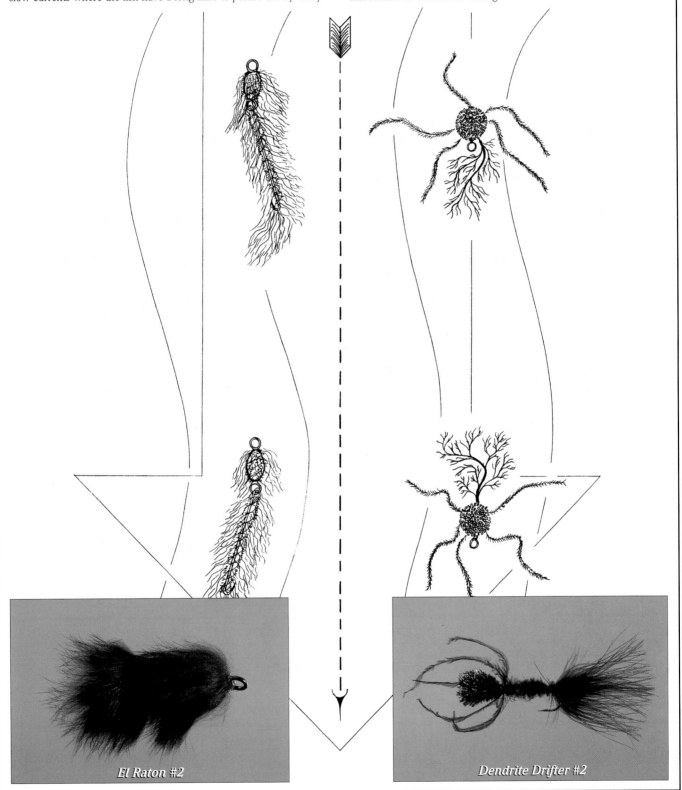

El Raton #2

Dendrite Drifter #2

Hinged Fly

A hinged fly reaches its full potential in the presence of turbulence. In this environment a weighted fly that is hinged has a greater latitude of movement from one that is not. This movement occurs predominantly in the abdominal section of the fly and is usually up and down, or side to side.

In general, appendage flies are constructed to enhance an up-and-down action in appendage flies, a side-to-side action in undulate flies. A hinged fly, as you may recall, is only a skeleton, but it is a skeleton distinct enough to warrant its own category. It does not matter what is used to make this fly so long as the head section is shorter and heavier than the abdomen. In almost every circumstance, this type of fly is used in the floor of the river where it can be presented moving with turbulent current. Any species of fish will take this type of fly and it is one of the few that will activate the surge of a chinook. Slots, pockets, and buckets are rooms where this fly does particularly well, especially in cold green water. There is only one technique that makes this fly unique from the other techniques using weighted flies, it is a technique I call the dance.

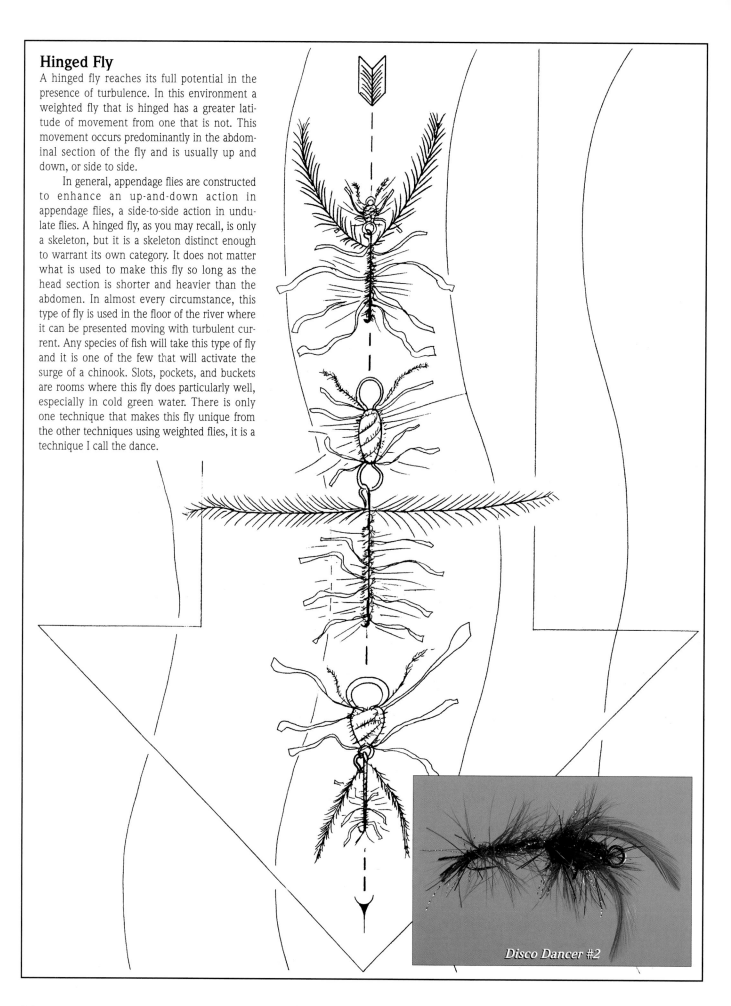

Disco Dancer #2

Chapter 12   **Underwater Rooms**

In rivers of mountainous regions such as the Northwest there are many kinds of underwater rooms where the angler may find fish. Each species of fish will hold in different kinds of rooms and prefer specific lies within each room. In large rooms such as pools and deep holes all species of fish may be present, but in other kinds of rooms the angler will find only one species. In general, brown trout and bulls will be found in only large rooms where they can sulk and wait for a big meal. Residential rainbow, cutthroat, and brook trout however, will establish themselves anywhere they can feed yet rest with security. Migratory fish such as salmon, sea-run cutthroat, and steelhead will lie wherever and whenever the configuration of the main channel causes them to pause before moving on, such as a natural obstacle (such as a rapid,) where they get stuck during low water (such as a pocket) or where it offers a respite after an exertion (such as a tailout.)

On the following pages there are a series of underwater rooms described and illustrated to help the angler develop a vocabulary. This vocabulary derives its meaning from three sources, the species of fish, the hydrodynamics of the fly, and the casting position of the fisherman. This vocabulary will enable the angler to visualize the river environment so that he or she can match the right type of fly and technique to the river environment and its underwater rooms. These rooms are described on the following pages. They are separated into four basic categories–large, linear, flat, and small rooms.

Large Rooms

Pools

The most common type of underwater room the angler will encounter in the Northwest is the typical pool. Technically, the definition of a pool is a deep, still spot in a river, but in the theater of angling it is much more than that. It is a distinct type of underwater room composed of many types of hydro-environments. It possesses a liquid anatomy. A typical pool will consist of the head, body, and tail. Each of these parts may contain seams and eddies.

Due to the fact that pools are a composite of many different hydro-environments, there is not any single technique or fly that can be used to cover the entire pool. Some pools might be amenable to virtually every application, while others may encourage the angler to use only one or two. It is requisite that the angler review the following descriptions of underwater rooms and applications to determine which technique and fly would be suitable to fish the various parts of a pool.

In general, the shallow head of a pool, one to four feet in depth, should be fished with a fin fly if the angler is able to position him or herself above the lie, or sometimes it can be fished with a waking fly if he or she can present the fly in front of the fish. In the deeper sections of the head, water four to six feet in depth, a hinged appendage fly would be more appropriate. In most circumstances the body of a pool is usually best addressed with a weighted undulate fly, and the tail with a floating undulate fly.

Anatomy of a Pool

Head

The head of a pool is usually characterized by shallow rapids, one to two feet in depth, followed by little depressions, two to four feet in depth, and then by chop, three to six feet in depth. Moving steelhead and other migratory trout will lie in these depressions. The chop may also hold moving steelhead, and occasionally resident rainbow or brook trout. Running salmon will sometimes hold in these depressions or on the outer edge of this chop.

Body

The body of the pool usually occurs where the grade drops off abruptly and forms a deep cavity of eight to twelve feet. In general, rainbow, cutthroat, and brook trout will lie towards the front of the cavity, bulls in the center, and pooled steelhead and salmon in the back. If more than one species is present this will all change, e.g., salmon will push bulls and steelhead about, rainbow and cutthroat will avoid exposure to bulls. In any case, fish holding in these cavities are somewhat difficult to move to the fly.

Tail

The tail exists as part of the main channel of the pool. It begins where the river bed rises again and is usually one to six feet in depth. The end of the tail is often referred to as a "tailout" and is distinguished by a increase in velocity of the current and a smooth appearance of the surface of the river. If this tail is three feet deep or greater, migratory trout or steelhead will often lie in this type of water.

Seams

A seam in a river is like a vertical wall of water. It is not really an entity in itself but is the result of two kinds of water meeting. It usually occurs where current traveling down river abuts non-moving water, slower-moving water, or water moving in another direction. To be inside the seam is to be on the side of the wall with the main current. Migratory fish tend to hold on the inside of the seam and resident trout on the outside. Remember however, that trout are looking upstream and move into the main current to take a fly. Therefore most "ugly flies" should be drifted in the main current regardless of what species is being pursued. Dimple flies are an exception to this and should be presented on the outside edge of the seam.

Eddies

An eddy is water moving in a circular motion in opposition to the main current. It is usually adjacent to the main current and occurs behind large rocks or in the body of the pool. Water in an eddy often looks more level and still. Wherever the main current and an eddy meet there will be a seam. Most species of fish will not inhabit this part of the river but it is a unique environment. The glass-like surface serves as a window and visual conduit to the bottom. Anything that disrupts this surface will be readily seen and resident trout will sometimes rise to clean this window.

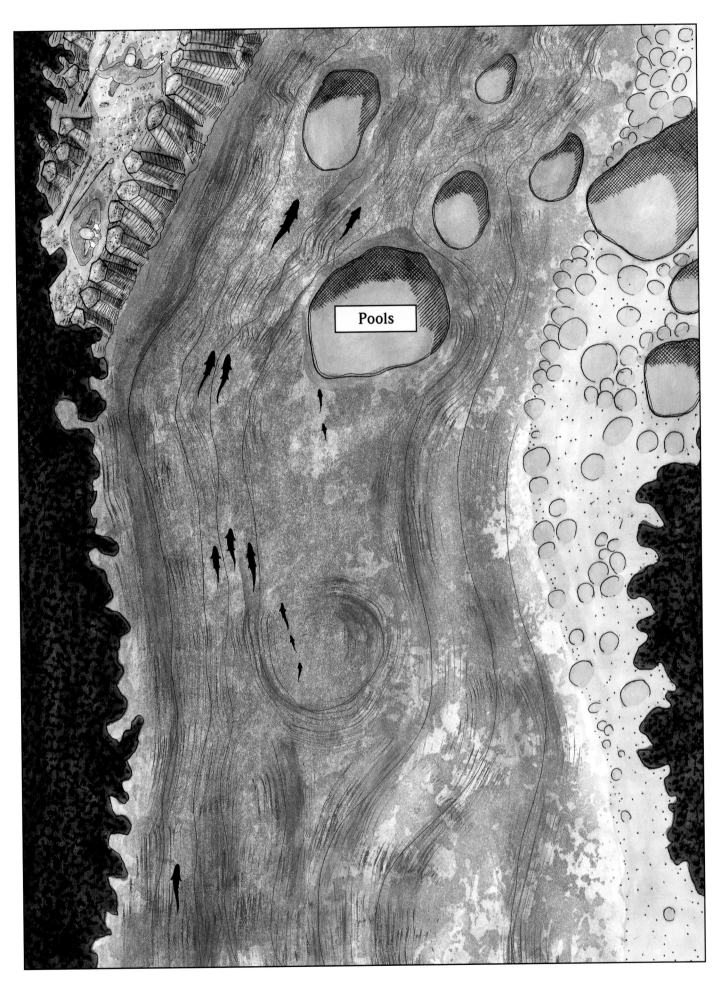

Pools

Direct Opposition
Undulate flies ("floating")

Although this technique sounds contrary to the concept of a dragless fly, it is actually based on going completely with the flow. To accomplish this, the fly angler positions him/herself behind the lie and casts the fly directly upstream and against the current. In this way, the fly, leader, and the line move in exactly the same path and at the same speed. While the fly is moving, the angler slowly lifts the rod and pulls in line to take up slack and prevent the line from entering faster or slower currents. Although this technique is extremely simple and easy, it is the reading of the water to place oneself in the correct position so that the current does all the work that takes experience.

An undulate fly, designed for use in the ceiling, works in places like the back of a pool or slow-moving trenches and tailouts. There are three basic reasons for using this technique. One, it is usually difficult to present a fly in the main channel in the back of the pool because of access and difficult currents. Two, a rise near the surface with little play in the line is easier to detect than a take on the bottom with lots of slack in the line. Three, migratory fish holding in these lies are very spooky, so an approach from behind will bother them less and a floating leader will not "line" them.

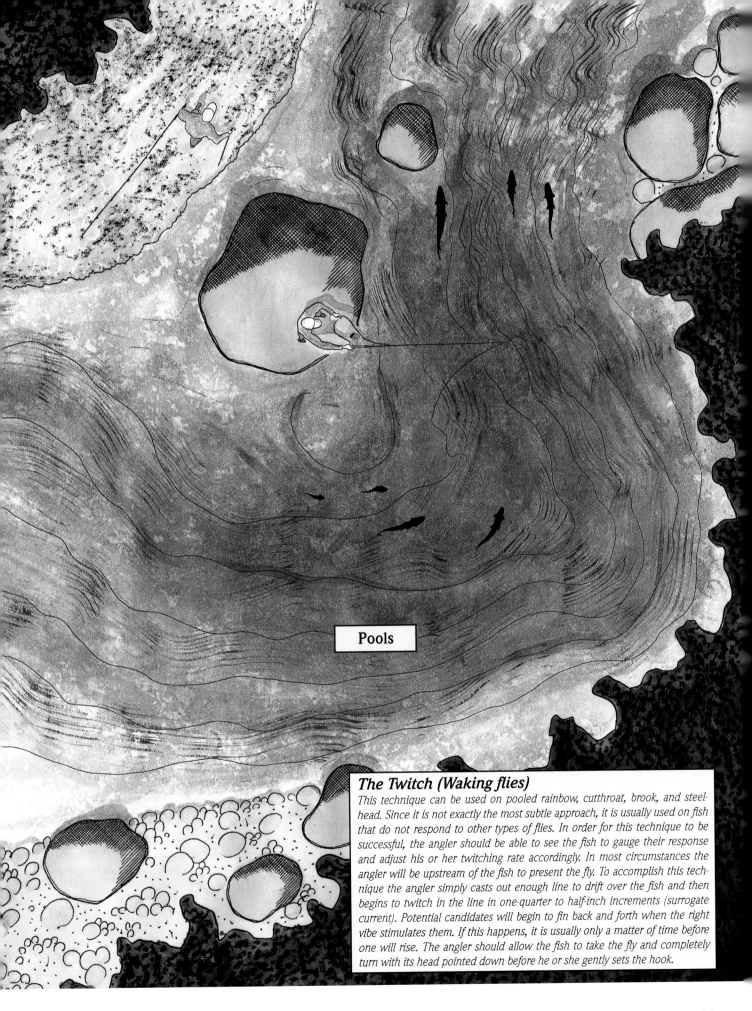

Pools

The Twitch (Waking flies)

This technique can be used on pooled rainbow, cutthroat, brook, and steel-head. Since it is not exactly the most subtle approach, it is usually used on fish that do not respond to other types of flies. In order for this technique to be successful, the angler should be able to see the fish to gauge their response and adjust his or her twitching rate accordingly. In most circumstances the angler will be upstream of the fish to present the fly. To accomplish this technique the angler simply casts out enough line to drift over the fish and then begins to twitch in the line in one-quarter to half-inch increments (surrogate current). Potential candidates will begin to fin back and forth when the right vibe stimulates them. If this happens, it is usually only a matter of time before one will rise. The angler should allow the fish to take the fly and completely turn with its head pointed down before he or she gently sets the hook.

Deep Holes

In a small river in the mountainous regions, a deep hole is only about ten to twelve feet in depth. This type of underwater room is usually characterized by a head that funnels into the semi-round body, and where the tail is broad and smooth. In most instances a fly is extremely hard to properly present in this environment due to the currents or lack of them. Also, fish "time" and fly "time" play a big role in this situation. In a deep hole, it behooves the angler to use a weighted fly, but because the fly is heavy it is difficult for the angler to present the fish with an animate image.

The angler is likely to encounter any type of fish in this type of underwater room, including chinook salmon. Indeed, chinook tend to gravitate to deep holes but in my experience are very reluctant to take a fly under these circumstances. The only major advantage to fishing a deep hole is the visual access it can provide. In many instances the angler will be able to see the fish and develop some technique that will tackle these fickle creatures.

Jigging (Appendage flies "sinking")

For some fly fishermen this technique would not be considered in any circumstance because of its connotations, (Only children or rednecks jig for fish; jigging only works in lakes; a jigged fly won't catch a trout; a trout is too noble a fish to take a jigged fly; it is an atrocity to jig for such a noble fish). In addition, some anglers believe that there is an inseparable and direct correlation between fly casting and fly fishing, if you are not doing one, you can't be doing the other. It took me almost twenty years of fly fishing for steelhead to realize the potential for this application. The technique is simple, it is finding the "spots" to apply the technique that is the challenge. In fact, no other technique will probably work in these spots. Like twitching, jigging (surrogate current) requires that the angler be able to see the fish and the fly to adjust the technique to produce the right action.

The perfect "spot" would have a deep hole, a big rock to stand on, and the correct angle of sun—and of course, fish. Another challenge to this type of angling arises when the fish charge the fly. Yes, they charge! When this happens the angler should do nothing until the fish grabs the fly and turns, at this point the angler should take up all the slack in the line until he or she feels the weight of the fish and then firmly set the hook.

Escarpments

Escarpments often form eddies due to the rock projection that confronts the current. The way this happens can manifest two different relationships between the current and the escarpment, which in turn affects where the fish lie. In general, if the main channel hugs the escarpment then so will steelhead and resident trout. In addition, these fish often become suspended (move off the bottom and hold next to the rock four to six feet below the surface) due to the physical structure of the rock and the security it offers. The other relationship occurs when the eddy is formed along the escarpment. In this event, resident trout and chinook will lie on the outside of the seam and steelhead will lie on the inside. In rare cases, usually in larger rivers, the counter-current caused by the eddy may create a lie where trout actually face downstream.

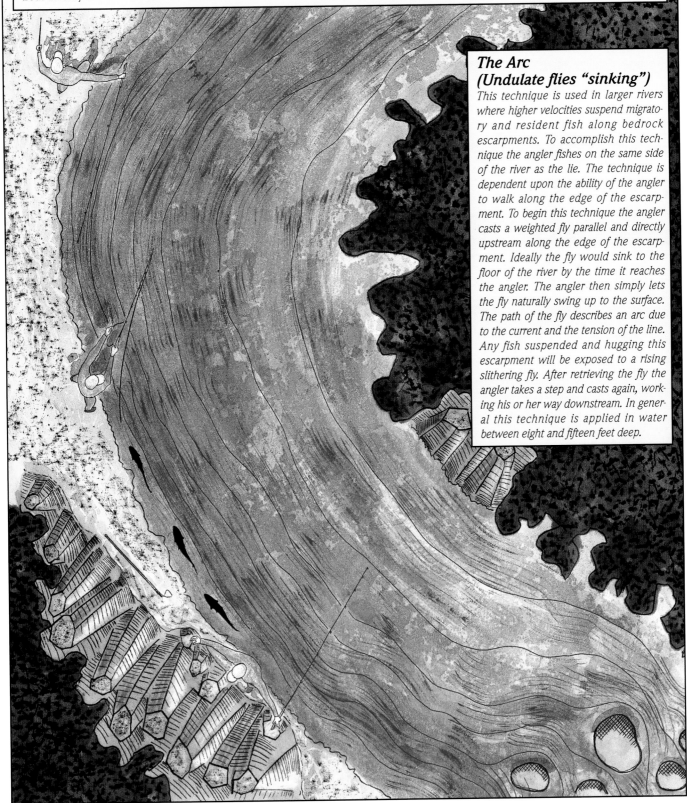

The Arc
(Undulate flies "sinking")

This technique is used in larger rivers where higher velocities suspend migratory and resident fish along bedrock escarpments. To accomplish this technique the angler fishes on the same side of the river as the lie. The technique is dependent upon the ability of the angler to walk along the edge of the escarpment. To begin this technique the angler casts a weighted fly parallel and directly upstream along the edge of the escarpment. Ideally the fly would sink to the floor of the river by the time it reaches the angler. The angler then simply lets the fly naturally swing up to the surface. The path of the fly describes an arc due to the current and the tension of the line. Any fish suspended and hugging this escarpment will be exposed to a rising slithering fly. After retrieving the fly the angler takes a step and casts again, working his or her way downstream. In general this technique is applied in water between eight and fifteen feet deep.

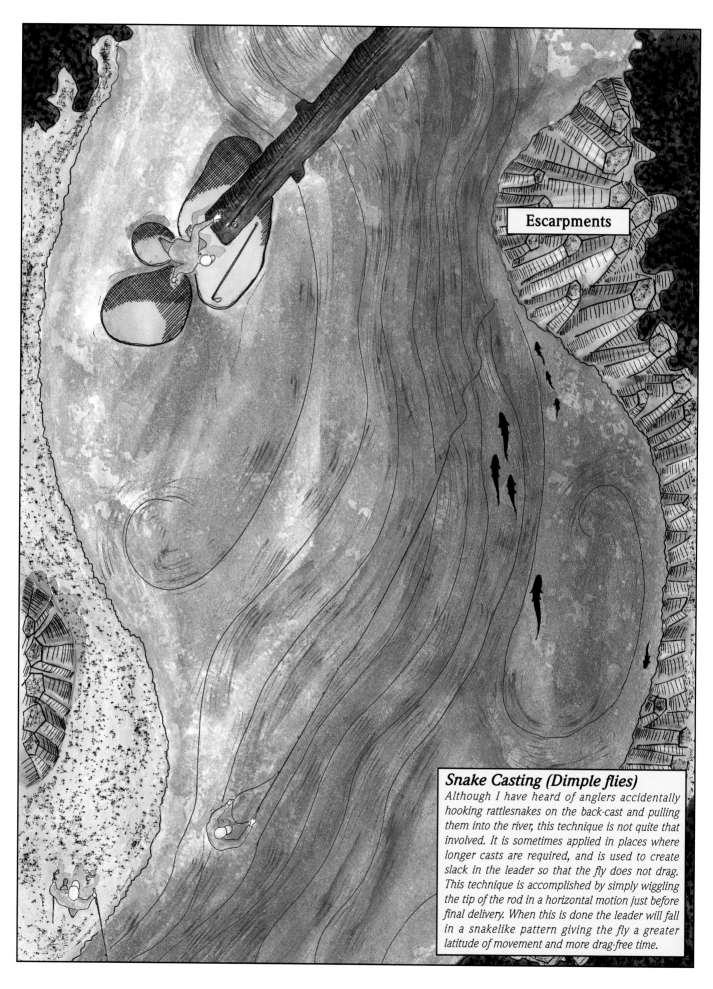

Escarpments

Snake Casting (Dimple flies)

Although I have heard of anglers accidentally hooking rattlesnakes on the back-cast and pulling them into the river, this technique is not quite that involved. It is sometimes applied in places where longer casts are required, and is used to create slack in the leader so that the fly does not drag. This technique is accomplished by simply wiggling the tip of the rod in a horizontal motion just before final delivery. When this is done the leader will fall in a snakelike pattern giving the fly a greater latitude of movement and more drag-free time.

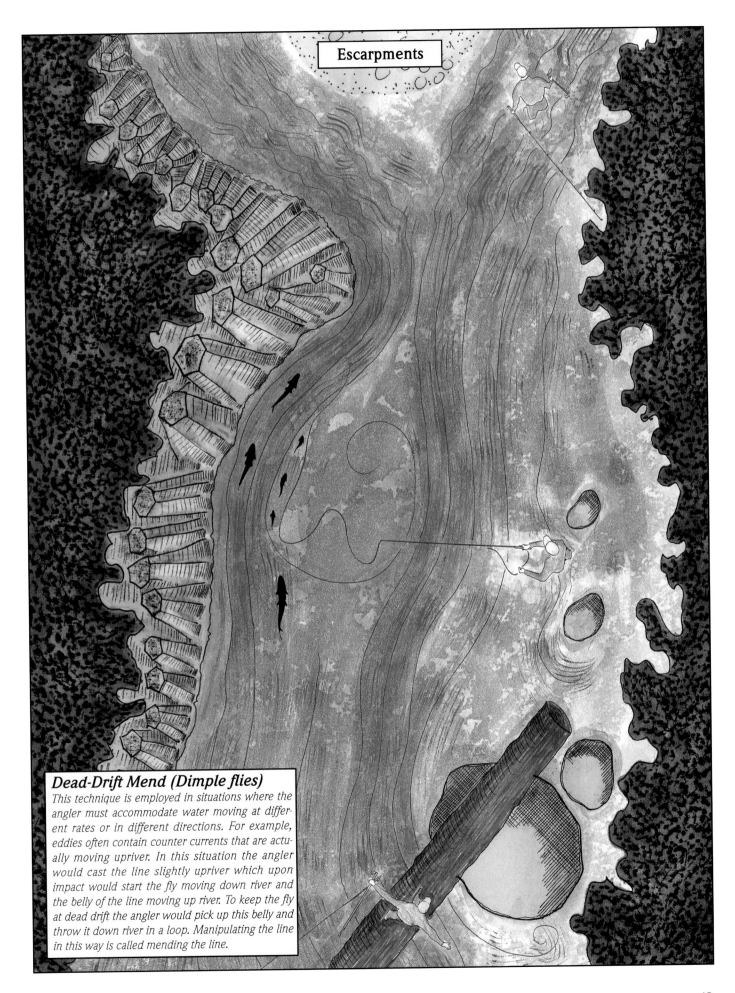

Dead-Drift Mend (Dimple flies)

This technique is employed in situations where the angler must accommodate water moving at different rates or in different directions. For example, eddies often contain counter currents that are actually moving upriver. In this situation the angler would cast the line slightly upriver which upon impact would start the fly moving down river and the belly of the line moving up river. To keep the fly at dead drift the angler would pick up this belly and throw it down river in a loop. Manipulating the line in this way is called mending the line.

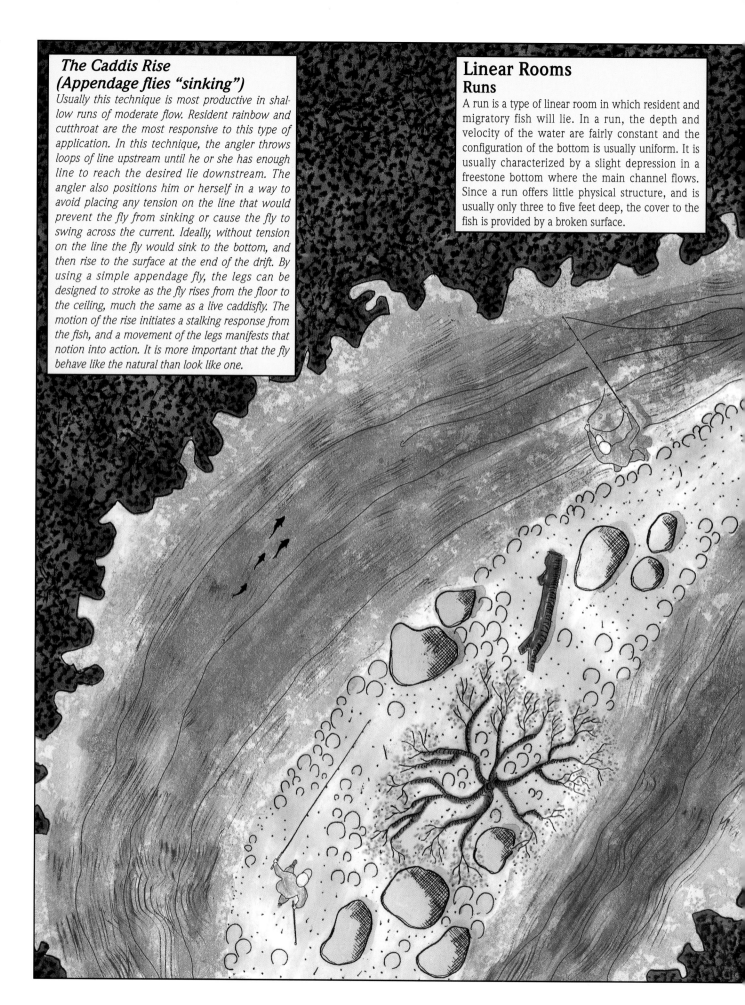

The Caddis Rise
(Appendage flies "sinking")

Usually this technique is most productive in shallow runs of moderate flow. Resident rainbow and cutthroat are the most responsive to this type of application. In this technique, the angler throws loops of line upstream until he or she has enough line to reach the desired lie downstream. The angler also positions him or herself in a way to avoid placing any tension on the line that would prevent the fly from sinking or cause the fly to swing across the current. Ideally, without tension on the line the fly would sink to the bottom, and then rise to the surface at the end of the drift. By using a simple appendage fly, the legs can be designed to stroke as the fly rises from the floor to the ceiling, much the same as a live caddisfly. The motion of the rise initiates a stalking response from the fish, and a movement of the legs manifests that notion into action. It is more important that the fly behave like the natural than look like one.

Linear Rooms
Runs

A run is a type of linear room in which resident and migratory fish will lie. In a run, the depth and velocity of the water are fairly constant and the configuration of the bottom is usually uniform. It is usually characterized by a slight depression in a freestone bottom where the main channel flows. Since a run offers little physical structure, and is usually only three to five feet deep, the cover to the fish is provided by a broken surface.

Runs

**Direct Opposition
(Appendage flies "floating")**
*The mechanics of this technique are almost identi-
cal to those used floating undulate flies in tailouts.
The difference is in the personality of the water
fished. Instead of the slow, smooth water undulate
flies are used in, appendage flies are often cast
into runs with a broken surface and enough energy
to move the parts of the fly.*

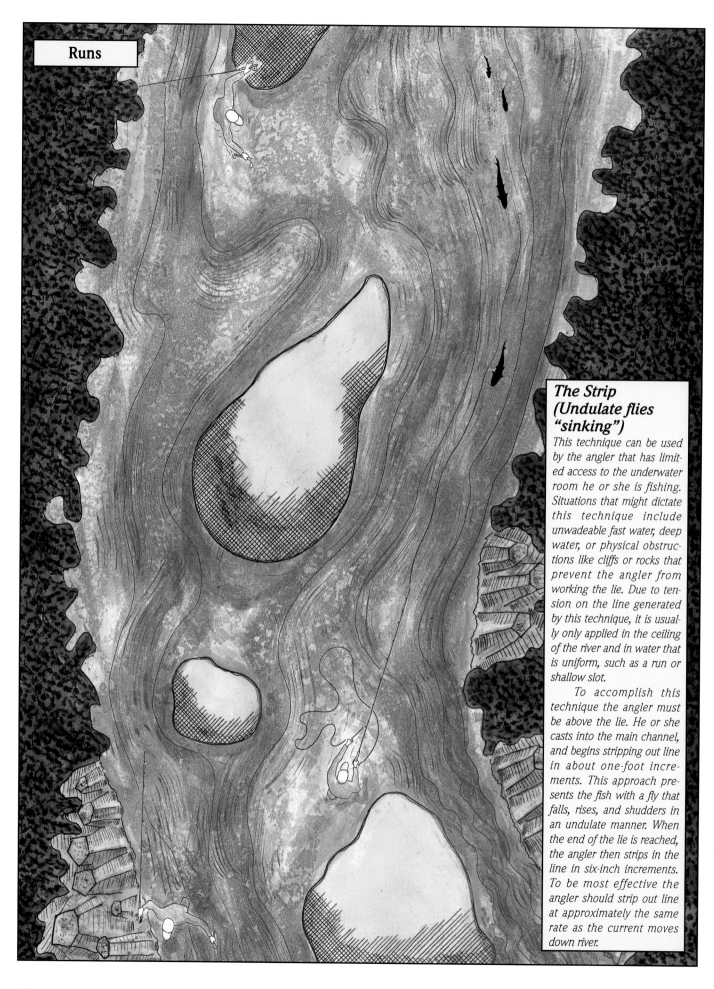

The Strip (Undulate flies "sinking")

This technique can be used by the angler that has limited access to the underwater room he or she is fishing. Situations that might dictate this technique include unwadeable fast water, deep water, or physical obstructions like cliffs or rocks that prevent the angler from working the lie. Due to tension on the line generated by this technique, it is usually only applied in the ceiling of the river and in water that is uniform, such as a run or shallow slot.

To accomplish this technique the angler must be above the lie. He or she casts into the main channel, and begins stripping out line in about one-foot increments. This approach presents the fish with a fly that falls, rises, and shudders in an undulate manner. When the end of the lie is reached, the angler then strips in the line in six-inch increments. To be most effective the angler should strip out line at approximately the same rate as the current moves down river.

Slots

Slots are linear rooms that occur in the main channel and are usually bordered by bedrock on at least one side. They are approximately four to eight feet deep, four to six feet in width, and vary in length. These rooms are avenues for migratory fish and do not often hold resident trout. Theoretically, any structure that is not part of the main channel (the route a migratory fish would take) cannot be called a slot.

Walking the Dog (Appendage flies "sinking")

This technique can be used to fish for any species in the floor of the river. It is a technique that utilizes the versatility and control of a floating line to enable the angler to stay in contact with the fly. It is a technique that is radically different from the ethereal presentation of a dimple fly. Indeed, it is not the most graceful form of fly fishing but it often works when nothing else will, especially when one is in pursuit of salmon or steelhead.

In most cases this technique only involves a short line of about ten to twenty feet and eight to twelve feet of leader. To properly present the fly to the fish, the angler positions him or herself immediately across the top of the lie and delivers the fly above and slightly across the main channel. With the upstream arm extended, and the rod held high, the angler then waits until the fly reaches the tip of the rod and gives it a little jerk to take the slack out of the line. At this point in time the fly should be within a foot of the bottom. With the slightest tension on the line, the angler stays in contact with the fly and follows it through the lie by switching hands, dropping the rod, and pointing the rod downstream. This method will help ensure that the fly stays in the river's floor for as long as possible. The angler "walks the dog". After casting once or twice, the angler then takes a step and casts again until the entire lie has been covered.

Slots

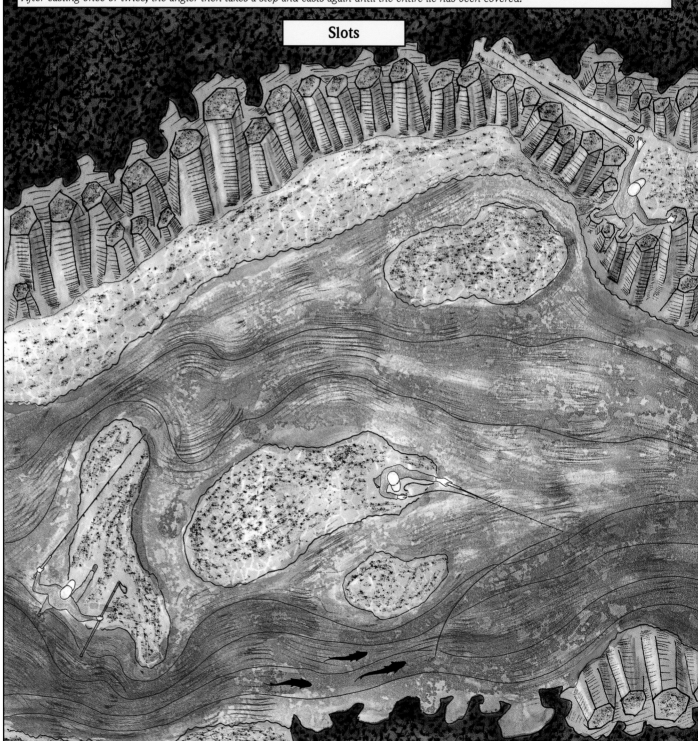

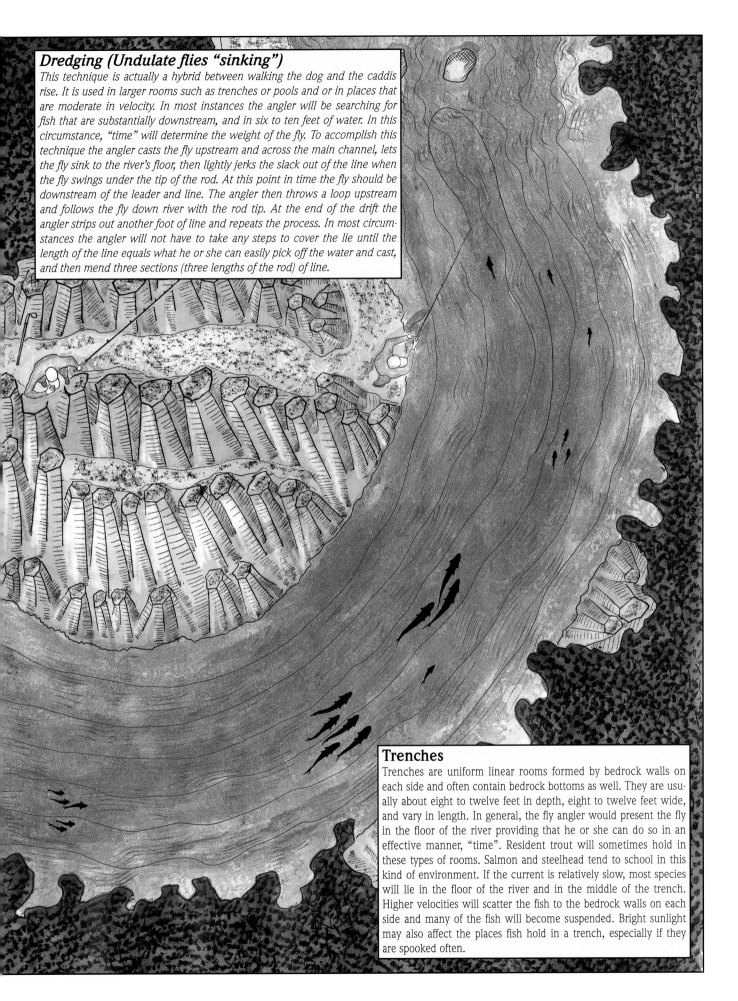

Dredging (Undulate flies "sinking")

This technique is actually a hybrid between walking the dog and the caddis rise. It is used in larger rooms such as trenches or pools and or in places that are moderate in velocity. In most instances the angler will be searching for fish that are substantially downstream, and in six to ten feet of water. In this circumstance, "time" will determine the weight of the fly. To accomplish this technique the angler casts the fly upstream and across the main channel, lets the fly sink to the river's floor, then lightly jerks the slack out of the line when the fly swings under the tip of the rod. At this point in time the fly should be downstream of the leader and line. The angler then throws a loop upstream and follows the fly down river with the rod tip. At the end of the drift the angler strips out another foot of line and repeats the process. In most circumstances the angler will not have to take any steps to cover the lie until the length of the line equals what he or she can easily pick off the water and cast, and then mend three sections (three lengths of the rod) of line.

Trenches

Trenches are uniform linear rooms formed by bedrock walls on each side and often contain bedrock bottoms as well. They are usually about eight to twelve feet in depth, eight to twelve feet wide, and vary in length. In general, the fly angler would present the fly in the floor of the river providing that he or she can do so in an effective manner, "time". Resident trout will sometimes hold in these types of rooms. Salmon and steelhead tend to school in this kind of environment. If the current is relatively slow, most species will lie in the floor of the river and in the middle of the trench. Higher velocities will scatter the fish to the bedrock walls on each side and many of the fish will become suspended. Bright sunlight may also affect the places fish hold in a trench, especially if they are spooked often.

Flat Rooms
Terraces

In most instances a terrace occurs immediately above a deep hole or trench. It is usually caused by a shallow bedrock shelf that runs perpendicular to the current. When the water flows over this shelf, the room created is uniform in its velocity and depth. Most terraces will be only about two to four feet deep. This type of underwater room is usually void of resident trout. Steelhead and other migratory fish will rest in this type of room and may become trapped until the next rain or rise in the water level.

The Upstream Loop (Waking flies)

In complete contrast to the dimple fly, which is cast to perform upstream, the waking fly is cast to perform downstream. To obtain maximum effectiveness from a waking fly, the angler should position him or herself above a bend or terrace and cast slightly across the rapids and then pull the fly into the main current while mending successive loops upstream. Once the angler has about twenty feet of line up stream in a straight line he or she can then let the line drift directly down with the current. The angler is presenting the fish with a dragless fly at this part of the application. When the fly reaches the end of this drift and begins to skate, the angler leads and follows the fly across the lie. With steelhead or sea-run cutthroat the most likely time of a savage strike occurs as the waking fly approaches the seam. With resident trout the take occurs on the slack-water side of the seam. The biggest problem with this type of fishing happens when the fish takes the fly. Invariably, the average angler will jerk the fly out of the fish's grasp when he or she feels the bite. This unfortunate occurrence can be overcome by either hesitating and dropping the rod when the fish strikes or by using about fifty feet of line which will provide enough play in the line to accommodate a short take.

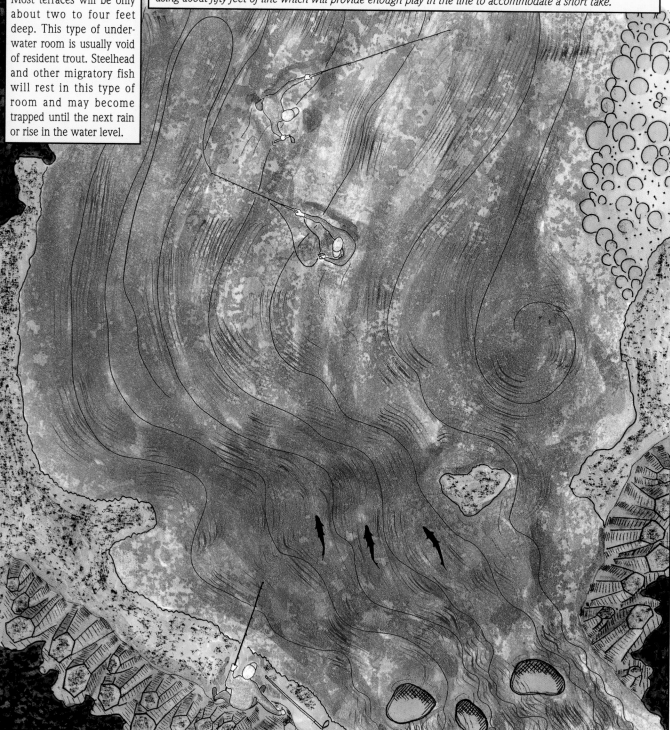

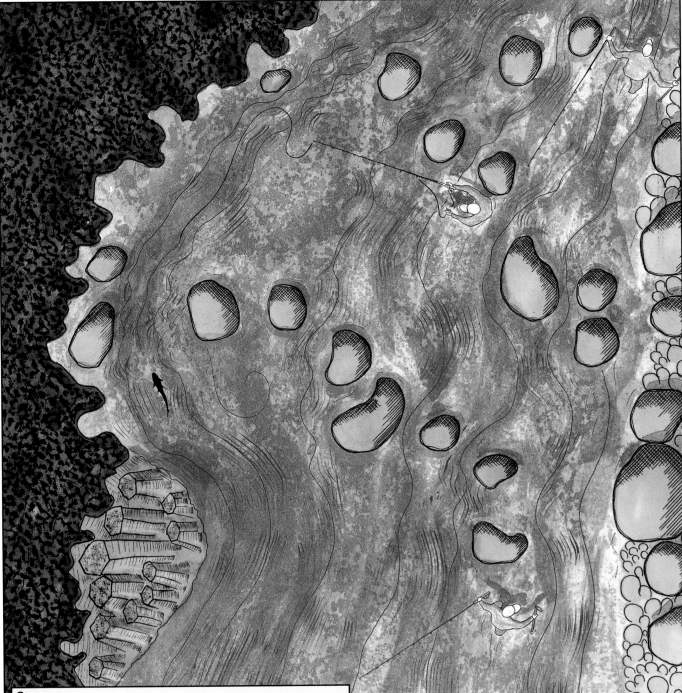

Steps

In general, steps are a freestone creation, being only about two to three feet deep, and usually occurring where the river gradually drops from one big pool to another. Obviously they provide a brief respite for any migratory fish that might be running and are easily probed with a floating line. Resident trout do not occupy this kind of water. Salmon will lie in steps, but due to the type of flies used in this situation, salmon rarely grab them.

Commentary

In steps and other shallow lies, most fly fishermen will bypass these opportunities because they do not see any fish and because most of them associate big fish with "big water". It is hard to believe but a three-foot fish can lay in one foot of running water, and be invisible. The average angler would not know the fish was there unless it either moved and flashed, or yanked the rod out of his or her hand.

The Reach Cast (Fin flies)

Essentially the reach cast is a technique that places a mend in the line while it is still in the air. It is most often used when fishing downstream and where the angler is above and to the side of the lie. Using this cast the angler can place both fly and about twenty feet of line parallel to and within the current flow. To accomplish this task the angler false casts at about a thirty-degree angle to the current and five to ten feet beyond the target. Upon final delivery, the angler reaches upstream. This movement in the rod places the line at dead drift when it hits the water. With experience this cast eventually evolves into a motion where the angler's arm stops momentarily and moves the rod backward, sideways, and up in a comma shape. In contrast to a normal cast (where the fly and line turn over) this motion causes the fly and line to turn under and straighten out before it lands.

Bends

Although many kinds of lies might be characterized by a bend or change of direction in the river, there is something unique about a bend that makes it distinct from other underwater rooms. It is not what it has, but what it hasn't. In general, it does not have a prominent main channel, bedrock bottom, or deep body. It is usually characterized by a rapids that drop over a sill into a head that is fairly uniform and constant. Normally the bottom is freestone two to six feet deep. Rainbow, cutthroat, brown, and brook may lie in this type of room, but bulls would probably not be found in such a place. For the fly fisherman a bend reaches its prime when the water rises. In these circumstances the steelhead begin moving upriver and tend to lie towards the head of the bend. A situation that enables the fly fisherman to search for these explosive creatures with one of the most effective tools in the world of angling–the fly and the floating line.

Modified Greased Line (Fin flies)

Although this technique is mechanically performed in the greased line tradition, it presents the fly in a way that is completely contrary. Originally the greased-line technique was developed for broad, shallow, and slow rivers and it presented the fish with a drag-free, sideways view of the fly. Most of the flies used were lightly dressed to achieve this type of presentation.

In the steep gradients of mountainous regions, a fin fly can be used in a radically different way using the modified greased line. This technique can be used in shallow runs or shallow bends when the angler's only viable approach is from the side. To begin this technique the angler casts the fly perpendicular to the current and into the main channel. Due to the planar surface of the fly it turns to orient itself in the current. This turning creates action in the fly. The angler lets the fly drift a short distance and then mends the line downstream. This mend serves two functions, first it keeps the fly in the main current and prevents it from swinging into the slack water. Second, it turns the fly sideways and reinstates the swimming action of the fly as it once again orients itself in the current.

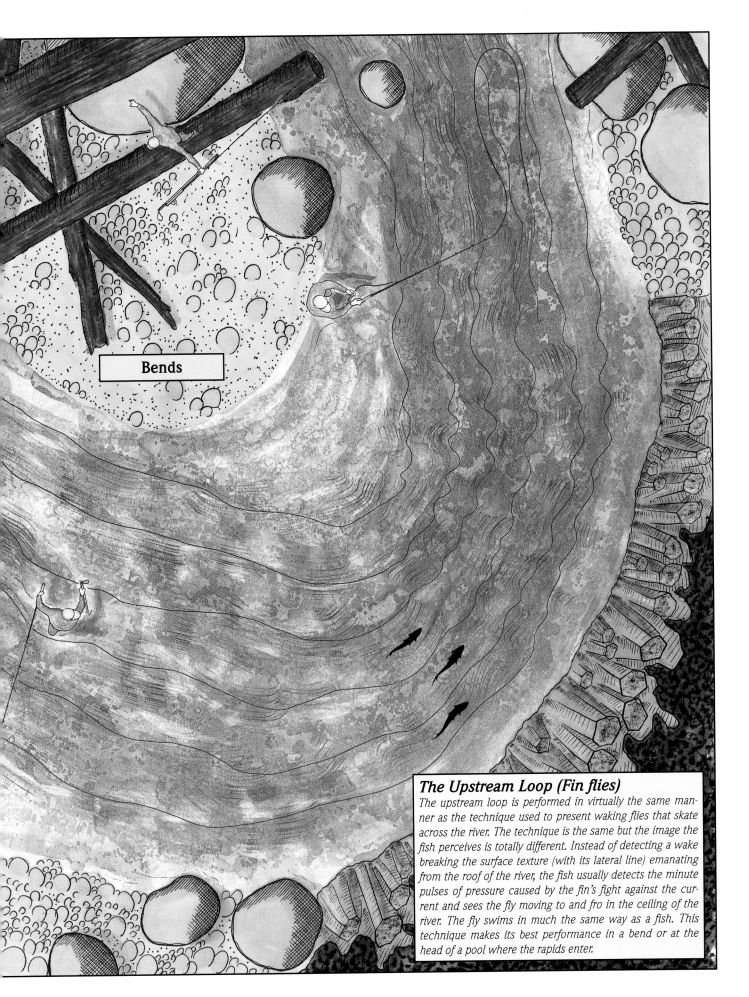

Bends

The Upstream Loop (Fin flies)

The upstream loop is performed in virtually the same manner as the technique used to present waking flies that skate across the river. The technique is the same but the image the fish perceives is totally different. Instead of detecting a wake breaking the surface texture (with its lateral line) emanating from the roof of the river, the fish usually detects the minute pulses of pressure caused by the fin's fight against the current and sees the fly moving to and fro in the ceiling of the river. The fly swims in much the same way as a fish. This technique makes its best performance in a bend or at the head of a pool where the rapids enter.

Bends

Reading Water

The Swing (Fin flies)

The swing is a technique that makes it necessary for the angler to be well above the lie he or she intends to fish. It works well in larger rivers in bends where the river is of a uniform depth of two to four feet. It is a simple technique that demands little technical skill but does require that the angler read the water and choose a position that will cause the fly to swing across the lie with as little side drag as possible. To accomplish this technique the angler simply casts the fly downstream at an angle of about thirty degrees and lets the fly swing on its own accord. Due to the fly's downstream movement that keeps pace with a relative lengthening of the line, and the fly's lateral movement due to the tension of the line, the fly swims across the river in a paced and natural way.

Small Rooms
Pockets

Pockets are small underwater rooms that are not often apparent from the surface of the river. They are either formed by craters in the bedrock or depressions in a freestone bottom. In order for the angler to discern these pockets, he or she must look virtually straight down into them or probe them with a wading staff. Summer reconnaissance when the water is low is a requisite for the serious steelhead fisherman. In some pockets the angler may also find resident rainbow or cutthroat. For the angler looking for bulls or browns this procedure is probably a waste of time. Caution, migratory runs of bulls or browns are an exception to this.

Roll Cast (Appendage flies "floating")

The roll cast is a technique the angler can employ in difficult conditions where he or she cannot get directly behind the lie or in front of it, and/or where a back cast is impossible. It is limited to a distance of about twenty feet and does not work well with bulky or heavy flies. In order to offer enough resistance for the line to form a loop, the fly and the last couple feet of the leader must be in contact with the water. To begin each cast the angler slowly pulls the fly through the water by raising the rod until the rod tip is directly overhead. At this point in time the rod should be perpendicular to the ground. The angler then assertively pushes the rod forward and down. This causes the line to form a loop, due to the fly stuck in the water. After enough momentum builds up, the loop will pull the fly out of the water and the line will flick forward and roll over.

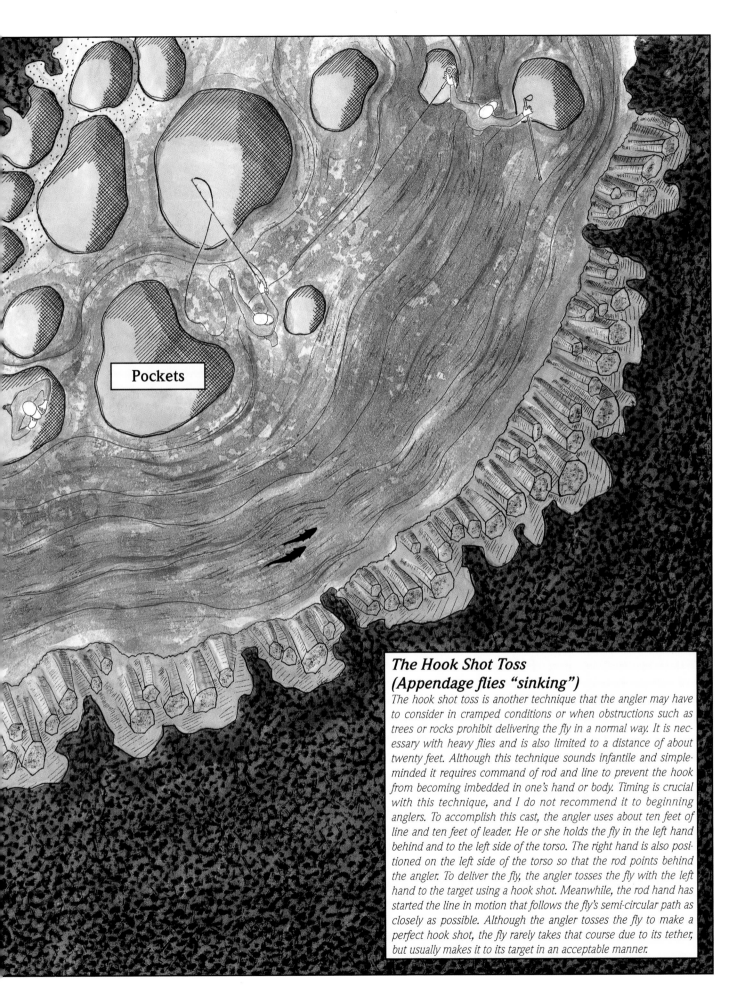

Pockets

The Hook Shot Toss
(Appendage flies "sinking")

The hook shot toss is another technique that the angler may have to consider in cramped conditions or when obstructions such as trees or rocks prohibit delivering the fly in a normal way. It is necessary with heavy flies and is also limited to a distance of about twenty feet. Although this technique sounds infantile and simple-minded it requires command of rod and line to prevent the hook from becoming imbedded in one's hand or body. Timing is crucial with this technique, and I do not recommend it to beginning anglers. To accomplish this cast, the angler uses about ten feet of line and ten feet of leader. He or she holds the fly in the left hand behind and to the left side of the torso. The right hand is also positioned on the left side of the torso so that the rod points behind the angler. To deliver the fly, the angler tosses the fly with the left hand to the target using a hook shot. Meanwhile, the rod hand has started the line in motion that follows the fly's semi-circular path as closely as possible. Although the angler tosses the fly to make a perfect hook shot, the fly rarely takes that course due to its tether, but usually makes it to its target in an acceptable manner.

Buckets

The main feature that distinguishes a bucket from a pocket is the way the water enters this type of room. In a bucket, the water appears to pour over a lip and into a tangible container. Most of the water flows over this type of room instead of through it. Also, a bucket is usually associated with some type of bedrock formation. Pockets on the other hand are more likely to occur in braided stream channels with lots of boulders and the current tends to flow directly through these types of rooms. Resident trout such as rainbow, cutthroat, and brook can be found in these types of rooms, but buckets reveal their full potential when the angler is after chinook or steelhead. Whenever a fly drops in on these fish and does a little shuffle, the hoe-down is about to begin!

The Dance (Hinged flies)

This technique is actually a manifestation of walking the dog and is not a completely separate entity unto itself. It is worth mentioning however because after years of observation I have seen it seduce many salmon and steelhead. In order to perform this technique the angler should use a hinged-appendage fly whose abdomen is designed to move up and down. This technique works best in buckets or where the water pours into a room. To begin this technique the angler casts the fly as he or she would when walking the dog, but does not jerk the slack out of the line. Instead, the angler lets the fly fall into the room with the rod held high. As the hinged fly falls, there exists a difference in weight between the head and abdomen (as there should be). This causes the head to fall first and the abdomen to ride high. When the fly comes under tension from the line, the fly stops and the head pulls up and the abdomen swings down. The whole ensemble resembles a kind of dance. Ninety percent of the time this is the very instant a fish will reach out and grab the fly. FANDANGO!

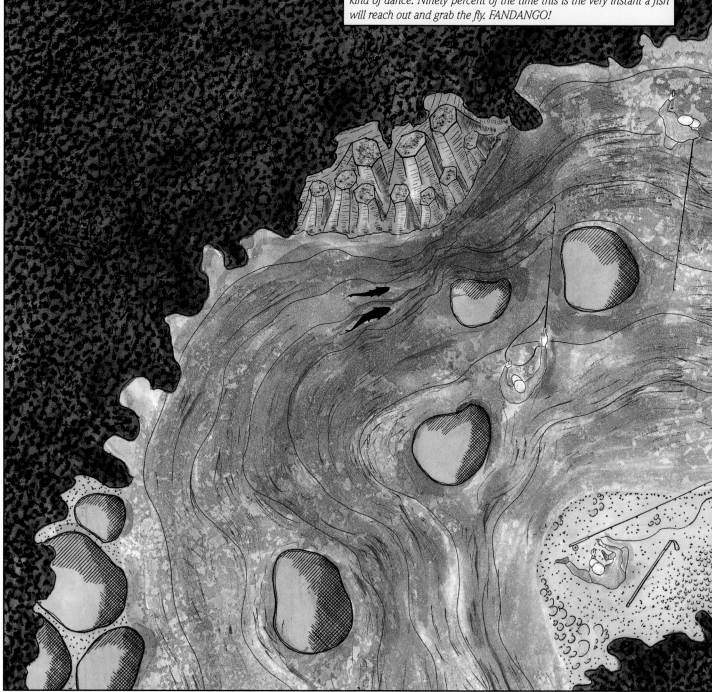

Direct Opposition (Dimple Flies)

The mechanics of this technique are almost identical to those of appendage flies when the angler wants to fish a lie from behind. The difference is in the personality of the water fished. Instead of the broken water in runs appendage flies are suited for, dimple flies are most often used in the eddies or on the glass-like surfaces behind boulders.

Boulders

Technically a boulder is a rock, it is the room formed behind the rock, sometimes in front, that fly fishermen address when they fish boulders. In a stream of moderate size with low velocities, virtually all species of fish will lie somewhere behind the boulder. In big rivers with high velocities the fish may also lie in front of the boulder where the water compresses against the rock and forms a relative dead spot, a reprieve from the tug of the strong current. In a stream where food is abundant, and anglers scarce, big trout will make their home among even the most modest of boulders.

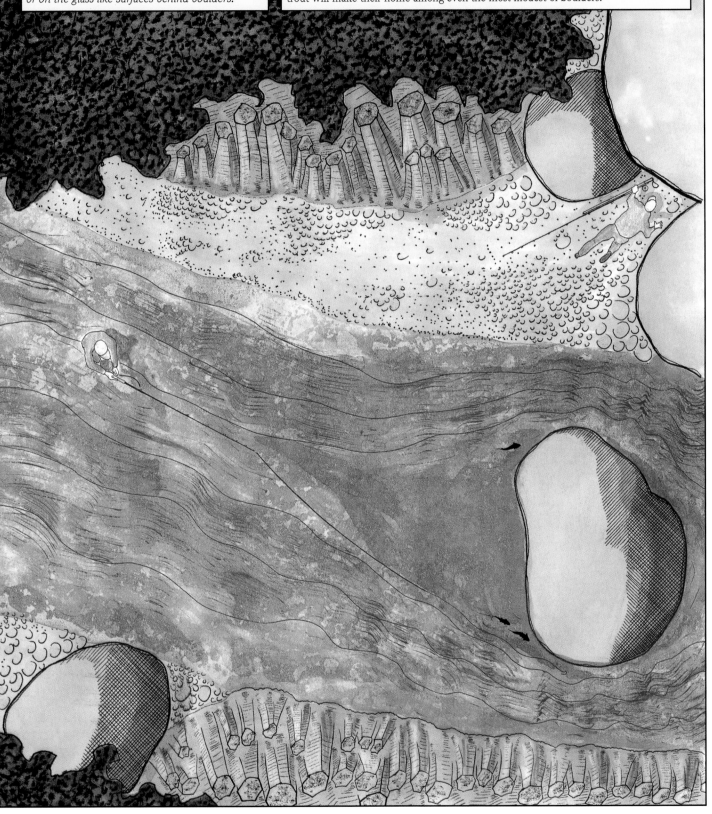

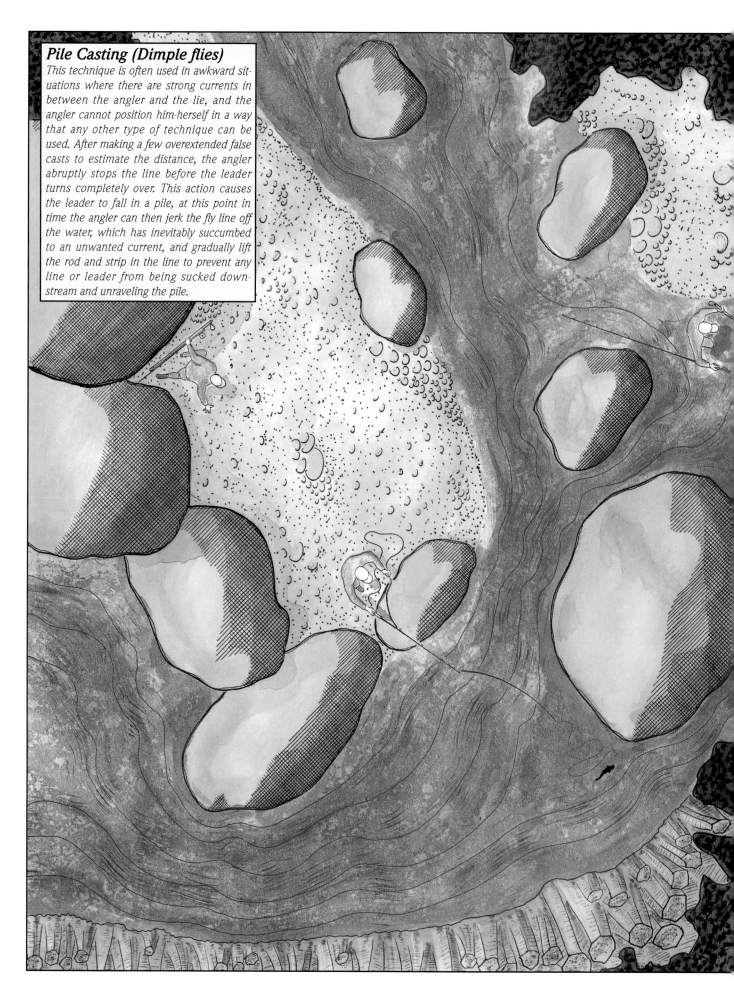

Pile Casting (Dimple flies)

This technique is often used in awkward situations where there are strong currents in between the angler and the lie, and the angler cannot position him-herself in a way that any other type of technique can be used. After making a few overextended false casts to estimate the distance, the angler abruptly stops the line before the leader turns completely over. This action causes the leader to fall in a pile, at this point in time the angler can then jerk the fly line off the water, which has inevitably succumbed to an unwanted current, and gradually lift the rod and strip in the line to prevent any line or leader from being sucked downstream and unraveling the pile.

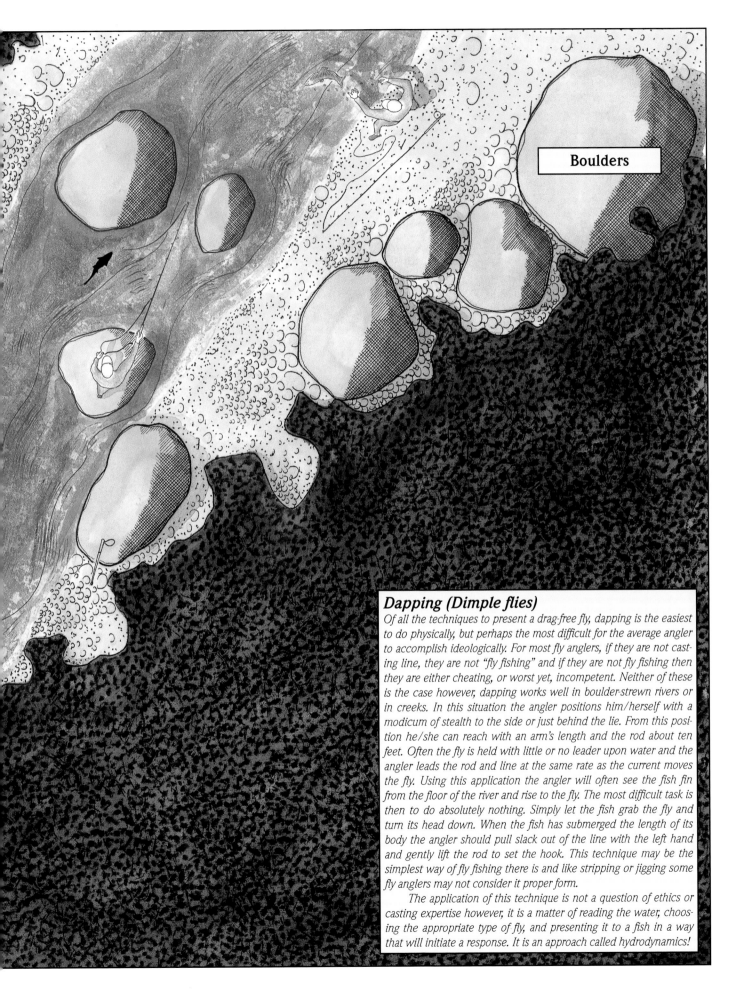

Boulders

Dapping (Dimple flies)

*Of all the techniques to present a drag-free fly, dapping is the easiest
to do physically, but perhaps the most difficult for the average angler
to accomplish ideologically. For most fly anglers, if they are not casting line, they are not "fly fishing" and if they are not fly fishing then
they are either cheating, or worst yet, incompetent. Neither of these
is the case however, dapping works well in boulder-strewn rivers or
in creeks. In this situation the angler positions him/herself with a
modicum of stealth to the side or just behind the lie. From this position he/she can reach with an arm's length and the rod about ten
feet. Often the fly is held with little or no leader upon water and the
angler leads the rod and line at the same rate as the current moves
the fly. Using this application the angler will often see the fish fin
from the floor of the river and rise to the fly. The most difficult task is
then to do absolutely nothing. Simply let the fish grab the fly and
turn its head down. When the fish has submerged the length of its
body the angler should pull slack out of the line with the left hand
and gently lift the rod to set the hook. This technique may be the
simplest way of fly fishing there is and like stripping or jigging some
fly anglers may not consider it proper form.*

*The application of this technique is not a question of ethics or
casting expertise however, it is a matter of reading the water, choos-
ing the appropriate type of fly, and presenting it to a fish in a way
that will initiate a response. It is an approach called hydrodynamics!*

The Beginning

Once the fly angler/tier has determined what species of fish he or she is going to pursue, the angler can then choose patterns for each situation. On the preceding pages I have shown which ugly flies I have designed and use, some of which are original, and some are very-close-to-established patterns. There is a difference between these patterns and many you can purchase in a store. However, in a store, flies are usually tied to either attract fish or fishermen. That is, they are made to look like a specific insect or they are made to appeal to the fishermen's understanding of beauty. Ugly flies, though, are constructed to interact and relate to the characteristics of moving water to produce an animate behavior. The image they present to the fish is dynamic; it is seen as a cinema (a sequence of events), instead of a snapshot (a moment frozen in time). The patterns I have shown are indeed effective, but the fly angler should not latch onto these patterns as the quintessential answer to successful fishing. These patterns are simply one possible expression of each type of "ugly fly". Any pattern that has been constructed with regard for the characteristics of moving water and a respect for the nature of materials will inevitably catch fish.

Caveat

In a well-stocked fly fishing shop the number of patterns can be staggering. If the angler were inclined to tackle a river from a hydrodynamic approach, he or she could probably purchase a repertoire of flies that would suffice.

YOUR FAVORITE FLY-TYING BOOK IS NOW AVAILABLE FOR USE ON YOUR COMPUTER!

THE FLY TIER'S BENCHSIDE REFERENCE
TO TECHNIQUES AND DRESSING STYLES

The Fly Tier's Benchside Reference to Techniques and Dressing Styles

AMATO BOOKS ON CD-ROM

• Using This CD-ROM
• Read The Book
• Install Software
• Visit Online Store

Ted **LEESON**   Jim **SCHOLLMEYER**

ACTUAL SCREEN SHOTS

$59.95

• Enlarge text and photos—print out or view on screen—for easier tying.
• Links highlighted for easy cross-referencing.
• Print out a particular method and hang it at a convenient, eye-level spot above your tying bench.
• See page 41 for complete description of *The Fly Tier's Benchside Reference.*
• Mac and PC format.

LARGEMOUTH BASS FLY-FISHING
Terry and Roxanne Wilson

The heart-stopping battles of largemouth bass have made them the most sought-after warmwater game fish in North America.

The pursuit of largemouth bass is nothing like dropping a tiny bit of feathers on the water's surface anticipating the delicate touch of a brightly colored fish. It's lobbing a heavy fly into weeds where it's slammed by a predator capable of jerking the rod from the angler's hands. This book includes: understanding bass habitat; approach, delivery, and fly animation; fishing the shallows; the vertical drop; fishing the mid-depths; going deep; time, weather, and locational patterns; plus seasonal and night fishing information; fly patterns; and more. 8 pages color, 6x9 inches, 160 pages.
ISBN: 1-57188-215-4   **SB: $16.00**

ONE MORE CAST
Albert Haas, Jr.

In this highly entertaining book, Al Haas tells tales of recent fishing adventures on legendary rivers, little-known streams, and on a vine-covered canal in Costa Rica's rain forest. In vivid detail, he also describes experiences from long ago.

Much of the book is about streamside discoveries. It is about the scene in fishing country and in country bars. About the role women have played in this fisherman's life and how much the outdoors has meant to four generations of his family.

Seasoned with wit and humor, it is sure to appeal to men and women who fish, yet has much to offer those readers who never fish but who wonder why so many others do.
B&W. 6x9 inches, 152 pages. **ISBN: 1-57188-224-3 HB: $24.00**

SALTWATER FLY-FISHING FROM MAINE TO TEXAS
Edited by Don Phillips

The sport of saltwater fly fishing continues to grow, the challenge and fun had hooking these large, strong, and fast species is just too irresistible. Includes: • where in the sea to find these fish • what they eat • most productive flies • which techniques are most productive • what tackle to use • what time of year is best to plan a trip • species • how to find the hotspots in unfamiliar waters • how to find a local guide, restaurant, shop, rentals • and much more.

Forty-three hot destinations for all saltwater species in the Northeast, Atlantic States, Florida, and the Gulf States are covered. Each destination is handled by a top guide in that area who answers the above questions, and more. That way you are sure to get extremely accurate information from those people who know the fisheries best. B&W w/16 full-color pages, 8 1/2 x 11 inches, 133 pages. **ISBN: 1-57188-252-9 SB: $22.00**
ISBN: 1-57188-254-5 HB: $35.00

Local guides describe their homewaters and 275 of their favorite fly patterns

GUIDE TO FLY FISHING KNOTS
Larry V. Notley • Foreword by Flip Pallot

Guide To FLY FISHING KNOTS

The single most important connection between a fisherman and a fish is a properly tied knot. This book is helpful, instructive, easy to understand, and will help you bring more of your catch to the net. Larry includes: parts of your line; IGFA line test; tippet to fly size chart; knot-tying tips; terminology; knot applications; and of course, step-by-step instruction for joining lines, lines to flies, loop knots, dropper knots, and yarn indicator knots. Also included are basic fresh- and saltwater leaders and trout and panfish leaders. Twenty different knots are covered with concise text and simple, clear illustrations showing each step. These knots offer a solid base for your knot-tying arsenal. So whether you fish salt water or fresh, this pocket-size book is perfect for your vest, boat, car, or tube.
B&W. 3 1/2 x 7 inches, 32 pages.   **ISBN: 1-57188-183-2 SB: $4.95**

STALKING WESTERN TROUT
Neale Streeks

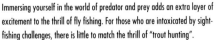

Immersing yourself in the world of predator and prey adds an extra layer of excitement to the thrill of fly fishing. For those who are intoxicated by sight-fishing challenges, there is little to match the thrill of "trout hunting".

In *Stalking Western Trout*, Neale Streeks, provides great detail on: the trout's shallow-water world, all you need to know about the trout's habits and its habitat; how and where to look for rising trout; reading riseforms, spotting subsurface trout; boat stalking, including techniques from your boat, seasons, hatches, and flies, hatch charts and matching fly patterns; and sight-fishing for various species in various water types, including salt water. Full color, 8 1/2 x 11 inches, 64 pages.
ISBN: 1-57188-207-3 SB: $15.95

FROM FIELD TO FLY: THE FLY TIER'S GUIDE TO SKINNING AND PRESERVING WILD GAME
Scott J. Seymour

From Field To Fly

If you enjoy the thrill of catching a fish on a fly of your own making, this book will take you one step further—preparing the materials you use to create those flies! *From Field To Fly* was written for the fly tier looking for a resource to help prepare and preserve wild game suitable for the vise.

Scott covers techniques for preparing: birds; upland game birds; waterfowl; small game; deer and other large game; and includes identifying feathers, tools and products you'll need, fly patterns, game laws, and more. So, go ahead, take that final step and harvest your own materials, *From Field To Fly* will show you how. That giant trout you catch will be all the more rewarding.

Full color, 8 1/2 x 11; 40 pages.   **ISBN: 1-57188-205-7 SB: $9.95**

STEELHEAD FLY FISHING AND FLIES
Trey Combs

The classic book on steelhead fly fishing and fly tying. Contains over 100,000 words on the subject. Chapters discuss geographical distribution of the runs and timing, early development of steelhead fly fishing and fly patterns, steelhead fly-fishing techniques and tackle. Over 200 steelhead flies are shown actual size and in color along with tying instructions and where and when they were originated and how fished. 90 photos and illustrations show how to fish the various techniques, read water, and tie correct knots. Beautiful book necessary for anyone interested in fly fishing for steelhead. 8 1/2 x 11 inches, 118 pages.

SB: $19.95   **ISBN: 0-936608-03-X**

FISHING JOURNAL: ANGLING LEGACY

Write, for future generations, about yourself and the stream. Use this attractive hard-bound book to record your days on the water for future use by yourself, relatives, or friends. It will become a treasured family document as it is handed down through your family. Each printed page contains spaces for entries such as: location, companion, weather, water conditions, fishing equipment, hatches, flies or lures, special fish sizes, species, etc. In addition there is much lined space for trip observations—what future readers will especially enjoy. Wouldn't you have liked to have read your grandfather's fishing journal? Start yours now! With ribbon and round back case binding, 6 x 9 inches, 240 pages.

HB: $19.95   **ISBN: 1-57188-211-1**

HATCH GUIDE FOR LAKES: Naturals and Their Imitations for Stillwater Trout Fishing
Jim Schollmeyer

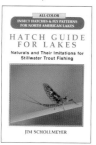

This "little lake Bible" organizes and explains lake types, how to read and fly fish them, and understand and imitate their aquatic insect life cycles—and nearby terrestrial insects. Next to each color insect photograph is a representative fly pattern. By carefully inspecting the lake for insects you can find the correct fly to use as shown in the book. *Hatch Guide for Lakes* is the golden key to unravelling one of fly fishing's last best-kept secrets. 4 x 5 inches, 162 pages.

HB: $21.95   **ISBN: 1-57188-038-0**

THE FISH BUM'S GUIDE TO CATCHING LARGER TROUT: AN ILLUSTRATED MANUAL ON STILLWATER TACTICS
Michael Croft

A brilliant explanation of how to fly fish still water, ponds, lakes, and reservoirs by a long-practiced expert. You will marvel at the inside information presented in a dramatic and hilarious drawing style. Valuable information about casting, reading water, lines, reels, rods, float equipment, flies, hatches, weather, structure. Hundreds of hand-drawn illustrations. 8 1/2 x 11 inches, 96 pages.

SB: $14.95   **ISBN: 1-57188-142-5**

DRY FLY FISHING
Dave Hughes

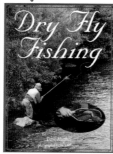

This beautifully written, all-color guide, will help make you a very competent dry-fly angler with chapters on: tackle, dry-fly selection, dry-fly casting techniques, fishing dry-flies on moving water and on lakes and ponds, hatches and matching patterns, and 60 of the best dries in color and with fly dressings. The information contained and attractive color presentation will really help you! 8 1/2 x 11 inches, 56 pages.

SB: $15.95   **ISBN: 1-878175-68-8**

HATCH GUIDE FOR WESTERN STREAMS
Jim Schollmeyer

Successful fishing on Western streams requires preparation—you need to know what insects are emerging, when and where, and which patterns best match them. Now, thanks to Jim Schollmeyer, the guessing is over.

Hatch Guide for Western Streams is the third in Jim's successful "Hatch Guide" series. Jim covers all you need for a productive trip on Western streams: water types you'll encounter; successful fishing techniques; identifying the major hatches, providing basic background information about these insects. Information is presented in a simple, clear manner. A full-color photograph of the natural is shown on the left-hand page, complete with its characteristics, habits and habitat; the right-hand page shows three flies to match the natural, including effective fishing techniques. 4 x 5 inches; full-color; 196 pages; fantastic photographs of naturals and flies.

SB: $19.95   **ISBN: 1-57188-109-3**

FLY FISHING FOR SUMMER STEELHEAD
John Shewey and Forrest Maxwell

This full-color book teaches you how to fly fish for magnificent, strong, acrobatic summer steelhead. Everything is covered: tackle, lines, rods, effective fly patterns and when to fish them, casting methods, reading water, wet-fly, greased line, skating, knots, wading, top 12 flies, fly tying etc. 8 1/2 x 11 inches, 48 pages.

SB: $15.95   **ISBN: 1-57188-028-3**

EVERYONE'S ILLUSTRATED GUIDE TO TROUT ON A FLY
R. Chris Halla • Illustrated by Michael Streff

Everyone's Illustrated Guide to Trout on a Fly is a must for every fly fisher's bookshelf. In the style of the phenomenally popular *Curtis Creek Manifesto*, this delightfully illustrated book gives basic information useful for all trout fly fishers, including: a history, proper clothing, miscellaneous necessities, rods, reels, lines, knots, casting techniques, trout food, best flies, reading water, tactics, safety, a description of trout, catch and release and conservation. With all this and more, *Everyone's Illustrated Guide to Trout on a Fly* is perfect for the beginning fly fisher in your life—and, who knows, you might learn a thing or two yourself! 8 1/2 x 11 inches, 96 pages.

SB: $12.95   **ISBN: 1-57188-098-4**

NYMPH FISHING
Dave Hughes

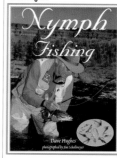

This masterful all-color, large format book by one of America's favorite angling writers will teach you what you need to know to fish nymphs effectively, with crisp text and dramatic color photos by Jim Schollmeyer. Color plates and dressings of author's favorite nymphs. All the techniques and methods learned here will guarantee that on the stream or lake your nymph imitation will be fishing right! 8 1/2 x 11 inches, 56 pages.

SB: $19.95   **ISBN: 1-57188-002-X**

WESTERN STEELHEAD FISHING GUIDE
Milt Keizer

Teaches you virtually all the techniques (from bait to fly) for steelhead fishing. Fly fishing section by Frank Amato. Dozens of drawings, maps and illustrations showing techniques, gear and rivers including in-depth chapters on California, Oregon, Washington, Idaho, and British Columbia that explain all the best rivers to fish and when, plus catch statistics. Comprehensive book about steelhead fishing and where to find the best rivers. 8 1/2 x 11 inches, 144 pages.

SB: $14.95   **ISBN: 0-936608-76-5**

ADVANCED FLY FISHING FOR STEELHEAD
Deke Meyer

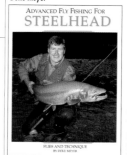

All-color book explains the most effective fly-fishing techniques for steelhead and the best contemporary flies to use. Chapters on: fly design; Spey flies; wet-flies; dry-flies; small-stream fishing; shooting heads; winter steelheading; two-handed rods; nymphing; deep drifting flies; and much more. Gorgeous book full of fly tying help and material preparation suggestions. Grand color plates of finest producing flies including pattern descriptions. With technique information and fly patterns presented you should be able to successfully fly fish for steelhead anywhere throughout the year. 8 1/2 x 11 inches, 160 pages, all color.

SB: $29.95   **ISBN: 1-878175-10-6**

HATCH GUIDE FOR NEW ENGLAND STREAMS
Thomas Ames, Jr.

New England's streams, and the insects and fish that inhabit them, have their own unique qualities. Their flowing waters support an amazing diversity of insect species from all of the major orders—in fact, at last count, Maine, alone, has 162 species of mayflies, the most of any state. Few, if any, books deal with the insects and life stages specific to New England, until now.

Hatch Guide to New England Streams, by professional photographer and "amateur entomology enthusiast" Thomas Ames, explores the insects of New England. The bulk of this book, however, deals with the insects and the best flies to imitate them. Tom's color photography of the naturals and their imitations is superb, making this book as beautiful as it is useful. A must for all New England fly-fishers! Full color. 4 1/8 x 6 1/8 inches, 272 pages; insect and fly plates.

SB: $19.95   **ISBN: 1-57188-210-3**
HB: $29.95   **ISBN: 1-57188-220-0**